Creating and Leading Children's Sermons
A Developmental Approach

When I was a child,
I spoke like a child,
I thought like a child,
I reasoned like a child.

—1 Corinthians 13:11

Creating and Leading Children's Sermons
A Developmental Approach

O. Suthern Sims, Jr.

SMYTH&HELWYS
PUBLISHING, INCORPORATED · MACON, GEORGIA

Smyth & Helwys Publishing, Inc.
6316 Peake Road
Macon, Georgia 31210-3960
1-800-747-3016
©1999 by Smyth & Helwys Publishing
All right reserved.
Printed in the United States of America.

O. Suthern Sims, Jr.

The paper used in this publication meets the minimum requirements of
American National Standard for Information Sciences—Permanence of
Paper for Printed Library Materials.
ANSI Z39.48–1984. (alk. paper)

Library of Congress Cataloging-in-Publication Data

Sims, O. Suthern.
    Creating and leading children's sermons:
    a developmental approach/
    O. Suthern Sims, Jr.
    p.   cm.
    Includes bibliographical references.
    1. Preaching to children.
    2. Children's sermons.
    3. Sermons, American.
    I. Title.
    BV4235.C4S55   1999
    251'.53—dc21   98-50822
                                                         CIP

ISBN 1-573132-266-1

Contents

For Mary

and our children
Suzanne and Tom,
David and Sabrina

and their children
David, Daniel, Mary Katherine,
Anne Marie and David Suthern

Introduction

As a preacher's kid growing up in the deep South, I spent a lot of time in church. In those formative years my father was my religious hero and the best preacher I ever heard. But, if I am honest, I have to confess that as a child, I really did not understand much he said from the pulpit. I did, however, gain a great deal by "just being there." The congregation affirmed me, and I knew I was loved and accepted by that community of believers. My faith foundation was constructed during those years. Out of this life experience I developed an empathy for children in church and a desire to make church meaningful and appropriate for them. This book is an attempt to satisfy that goal.

The children's sermon, an established time during the Sunday morning worship service devoted exclusively to children, is a practice that has grown and expanded into virtually every Christian denomination during the last 30 years. A special time for children during the Sunday worship hour takes many forms and involves different age groups depending upon the needs, purposes, and objectives of a particular church. Not everyone has endorsed the practice, however. Ferrol Sams writes,

> I was reared in an era when children should be seen and not heard. Nowhere was this more evident than on Sunday morning in church. It has been a trifle difficult, therefore, for me to adjust to the interruptions of ritual throughout our land called Children's Worship.[1]

Unfortunately, too many persons responsible for making presentations in "children's church" know little about how children develop physically, cognitively, and socially. They also lack an understanding of the historical place of children in the culture and have an inflated confidence in the American culture's current acceptance of the value of children.

Historically, children have not fared well. There is some evidence, for example, that the Greeks and Romans abused but valued children. In particular, if a male child was accepted by his family and showed promise in his ability to reason, he was considered a candidate for education and was thus valued to some degree. All younger children received little recognition.

During the Middle Ages there was little or no interest in education for the masses. Children were viewed simply as byproducts of the male-female union. The infant mortality rate was high, records of birth and death were nonexistent, and children, if they survived infancy, were often sold into slavery or sent to foster homes or monasteries. During the Dark Ages, children may have even been viewed as special examples of original sin. The term "sinful child" was often used to describe the children of this era. Children, therefore, needed to be controlled and molded by adults into adult roles, making them into miniature adults. They were dressed and treated as adults, worked as adults, and experienced the same stresses as adults.

It was not until the Reformation and Renaissance that childhood was recognized as a somewhat separate period in the human development paradigm. Specifically, during the late seventeenth century the British philosopher John Locke postulated that the mind of a child is like a "blank tablet" (*tabula rasa theory*) until life experiences provide "writing" to shape the destiny of the child. Locke's ideas fostered the notion of the "neutral child." During this period both parents and teachers came to realize that they, not some cloudy idea of original sin, were responsible for the outcomes of children's development.

But it was the 18th-century philosopher Jean-Jacques Rousseau who forcibly declared that children are separate from adults; they feel, think, and behave differently from adults. Furthermore, he believed that children are innately good and that society corrupts them. Rousseau said that children should be valued for who they are (children), not who they will become (adults). Since parental constraints and social restrictions would hinder physical, cognitive, and social growth and development, children should be left alone as long as possible to allow natural, positive characteristics to flourish. Rousseau ushered in the age of the "good child."

Then in the 19th century Sigmund Freud developed the concept of the "sensual child," based on the idea that a child's thoughts during the first 5 years of life are primarily sexual and the personality is developed simultaneously. He established the language of child development, the existence of the unconscious, the importance of early experiences, and the necessity of attachment between child and caregiver. Freud's child development theory dominated for more than half a century.

Following World War II, significant changes occurred around the world, especially in America. Males entered colleges and universities in unprecedented numbers, marriage was the interpersonal event of the day, and children were born in numbers that inspired the term "baby boom." Because of the post–World War II emphasis upon education and career advancement, children of the boomers were herded into beginner dance programs, music programs, math and science programs, and any kind of program that had to do with getting a jump on school performance.

Some human developmentalists have called the period from the late 1960s to the present the age of the "competent child." David Elkind defines the term competent child to mean the "hurried child," or "super kid." He further states that if children are competent, it follows that many of their caregivers believe it is acceptable or even desirable to "hurry" them in their developmental quest. Indeed, Elkind implies, if the culture believes children can be formally educated in and just out of the womb, then many parents and other caregivers may feel obligated to enroll very small children in complicated and abstract academic programs such as reading, math, science, and social studies.

In his book *The Hurried Child*, Elkind makes two major points concerning the competent child. First, parents who believe that children are competent to deal with the changes of life without parental supervision and support have devised a system of rationalization that permits them to continue to love their children, but excuses them from spending the time and energy required for their involvement in their children's childhood. In short, parents or caregivers do not have to feel guilty and anxious if they do not have time for their children. After all, the children are competent, so parents are not really needed that much! Second, the primary outcome for "hurried children" is stress. And stress in children leads to many of the outcomes experienced by adults who are anxious and stressed: disturbances in physical, cognitive, and social development.

Despite America's material wealth and social sophistication—which includes child labor laws, compulsory education laws, extensive social welfare consisting of medical programs benefiting children, free government printed materials on human developmental and childrearing issues, and thousands of articles and books on the subject of children's development and childrearing strategies—childhood is a trying, difficult, stressful, and more than occasionally dangerous time. Note the following statistics for a typical day in the lives of children in the United States in the 1990s:[2]

- 17,051 women get pregnant; 2,773 of these are teenagers.
- 1,106 teenagers have abortions.
- 372 teenagers miscarry.
- 1,295 teenagers give birth.
- 689 babies are born to women who have not had adequate prenatal care.

- 719 babies are born at low birth weight.
- 129 babies are born at very low birth weight.
- 67 babies die before they are 1 month old.
- 105 babies die before they are 1 year old.
- 27 children die from poverty.
- 10 children die from guns.
- 30 children are wounded by guns.
- 6 teenagers commit suicide.
- 35,000 children bring a gun to school.
- 7,742 teens become sexually active.
- 623 teenagers get syphilis or gonorrhea.
- 211 children are arrested for drug abuse.
- 437 children are arrested for drinking or drunken driving.
- 1,512 teenagers drop out of school.
- 1,849 children are abused or neglected.
- 3,288 children run away from home.
- 1,629 children are in adult jails.
- 2,556 children are born out of wedlock.
- 2,989 see their parents divorced.
- 34,285 people lose jobs.

Another indication of how well children fare in our society is found in *The Kids Count Data Book*, released annually from the Annie E. Casey Foundation, which ranks the fifty states and Washington, D.C. on ten indicators of childhood well-being. These indicators include infant mortality rate, child death rate, percent of teens who are high school drop-outs, percent of teens not attending school and not working, percent of children in poverty, percent of children living in single-parent homes, juvenile violent crime arrest rate, teen birth rate, rate of teen deaths by accident, homicide and suicide, and percent of low birth weight babies. For example, the 1997 *Kids Count Book* gives the following rankings from high to low:

- 1 New Hampshire
- 22 Virginia
- 39 Texas
- 45 Georgia
- 47 Florida
- 51 Washington, D.C.

In spite of America's affluence, political power, and educational opportunities, the children in our culture are far from being safe and feeling secure: 20% live in poverty; 20% go to bed hungry every night; millions are scared, abused, depressed, and stressed. Only 6 countries in the world allow for the execution of juveniles, and the U. S. is one of those! It is no wonder some child advocates believe that for many children in this country the Dark Ages are still present.

The comprehensive role of the church in the life of children is not within the scope of this study. However, the children's sermon as a small but important part of that role is. For a few brief moments every Sunday morning the church can minister to children in a way that can significantly impact their growth and development. By choosing developmentally appropriate materials, words, stories, and illustrations, the children's sermon presenter can share with children God's love for them and, in return, the congregation's acceptance of them as the children of God and the children of that fellowship of believers. Presenters of children's sermons should emphasize love, joy, sharing, forgiveness, peace, hope, security, safety, and cooperation. If presented in the language, context, and experiences children understand, children's sermons will effectively teach these and other concepts and attitudes of the church.

The purpose of this book is threefold. The first section gives guidelines for preparing children's sermons that communicate with children of various ages based on their physical, cognitive, and social development. The second section provides 60 model sermons developed according to the principles discussed in the first section, emphasizing general topics, "church words," and special days—all of which lay a faith foundation. The third section furnishes child development information and theory, children's sermon research survey results, and references that give credence to the importance of using appropriately developed children's sermons in worship. The material discussed in the third section is applied in the first two sections of the book.

Note

[1]Ferrol Sams, *The Passing* (Atlanta: Longstreet Press, 1988) 61.

[2]J. W. Santrock, *Children*, 5th ed. (Dubuque IA: Brown & Benchmark Publishers, 1997).

Acknowledgments

A concerted effort has been made to avoid direct quotations from writers. However, such could have occurred unintentionally. During the last 40 years of taking notes on human development, there has been scarce attention to footnoting. Therefore, apologies are offered in advance if material has been used without permission. Certainly, there is an indebtedness to the theorists and other authors in the field of human development for their concepts and perceptions, many of which have shaped my own eclectic views.

In addition to the many theorists and authors who have shaped my philosophy and content for this book, I owe appreciation to a cast of many who helped me produce the manuscript.

My thanks to Sally Sutton, Virginia Martin, and especially, Theresa Crowley for excellence in word processing, and to Penni Hartley for her skill with the preliminary graphics.

Much of the survey work and some of the information on developmental theories and faith development is the work of three very hard working graduate students at Mercer University: Juanita Lewis, Carol Maholski, and Angela Moliere.

I am indebted to Dean Anne Hathaway and the Mercer University School of Education for the sabbatical leave that provided me time to complete this project. There were individuals who spent countless hours reading the manuscript and offering valuable suggestions. Thanks to Ruth DuCharme, Cathryn Futral, Buddy Revels, Robert Richardson, Sara Powell, Bill Powell, and Paul Campbell. My list of "thank you's" would be incomplete without the names of my pediatric mentors, Elizabeth Patrenos, Edward Clark, Debbie West, and in particular Stuart Levi.

Finally, appreciation is expressed to my editor, Jackie Riley, whose insight and organizational skills contributed significantly to the outcome of this manuscript.

Preparing Children's Sermons

Connecting with Children

Seeing the world through the eyes of children is a magnificent experience. Children view life filled with a sense of wonder, awe, and curiosity. They have a seemingly innate desire to know, to discover, to investigate their surroundings, to learn what and why. This desire is as true about spiritual matters as it is about the physical world. Children want to know who God is and where God is. They want to know about the beginning and ending of the world, and they want to know that what adults tell them about God is true. Children demand answers to some of life's most difficult questions.

As they grow, children will raise questions regarding faith and what they hear during worship. The worship services children attend, therefore, should be carefully planned to welcome and include the children in ways they can understand. Worship experiences should be seen as corporate actions in which children are participants with adults, while recognizing that children will not perceive information on the same level and with the same understanding as adults. The very youngest children can gain meaning from worship, using their senses of sight, sound, smell, touch, and even the affective feelings that come from being in worship with their parents and church family. As children absorb the atmosphere of the worship experience, they store memories that may not yet be understood but that may be recalled at a later time with comprehension.

As children worship with the members of their church, the children are learning about God and simultaneously expressing their relationship to God. They must be allowed to interact with the gospel at their own level of understanding, recognizing that all people have different responses according to their individual stage of development. It is also important for children to be allowed to ask questions. Adults should, then, listen carefully for the meaning of the questions, answering in terms that are relevant to the experience of children. Questions are normal, and answers should be given in simple, kind, and truthful terms that can be easily translated into the life experiences of children.

One of the most important means of communication with children in worship today is the children's sermon. This simple yet complex instrument can be a potent way to include children in the service and to make them feel welcome as participants. It is more than a time to learn facts; it is a way to experience the insights of the Scripture. Those who use children's sermons effectively actually enhance the worship service by ministering to the entire worshiping body of believers while talking to the children in language they can understand.

Children are unique individuals and should neither be ignored during worship nor treated as "little adults." Communication with children should occur in authentic terms that relate to their stages of development and experiences. The task of those who teach children is to recognize and understand these stages and use appropriate methodologies, such as children's sermons, to minister effectively to them as individuals.

Children's sermons can make children feel welcome, foster a warm relationship between presenter and children, and teach biblical truths in simple terms. In addition, youth and adults in the congregation are "silent learners" who can usually benefit from children's sermons.

Presenters of children's sermons can better connect with children by understanding basic human developmental needs and applying effective communication skills. It is essential to keep in mind that:

• Both biology *and* environment influence overall development.

• Early experiences, social interactions, positive parent-child relationships, and moral development affect future development.

• Moral development is related to perception, memory, and judgment—all of which tend to be qualitative in nature.

• Developmental processes are contextually related, thereby requiring teaching slightly ahead of one's experiences and understanding.

• Self-image is important to development.

• Needs are useful in understanding motivation and behavior.

• The role of faith is a contributor to development.

• Behavior affects the environment; environment affects behavior.

• Behavior is frequently imitated by children; consequently, what one does in front of children is more important than what one says.

Awareness of these principles of human development can help presenters incorporate age- and language-appropriate lessons that incorporate concrete, familiar experiences.

Appropriate Language

While it is vital that children learn to use the language of faith, many of the problems associated with children's sermons may be attributed to the use of this language. The words used are often not within the understanding of children. It is possible to use metaphors, idiomatic speech, parables, and symbolism within children's sermons, but these forms of language are misused when the assumption is made that children have the same comprehension abilities and the same experiences as adults. Words familiar to adults are often not understood by children unless placed into concrete contexts. It takes practice and careful planning to share the language of faith on a level children can understand.

The cardinal sin in communicating with children is to assume they understand the meaning of adult words, phrases, and sentences. Even though the children may use the word "mother" and the presenter uses the same word, the meaning of "mother" is far richer in meaning to the presenter. The multiple meanings of the word come from the different experiences and contexts of the adult presenter.

Children can amaze us with their vocabularies, but it is a mistake to believe that just because they can use the word "essential" correctly in one context, they also understand when the presenter discusses the "essentialness of love in the Christian faith." That phrase contains at least four words that are bathed in abstractness: essential, love, Christian, and faith. In order to communicate effectively the meaning of these words to children, it is necessary to know what these words mean to them and in what context.

Communication theory teaches that in order to communicate effectively with another person, the "receiver" of the message must have the same meanings for the words, contexts, and experiences as the "sender." If this pairing is not present, the message is either misunderstood or not understood at all. This truth is never more evident than in children's sermons when the vocabulary of faith is often used by the presenter. And there is no vocabulary more abstract than that of the church.

It is also a mistake to assume that the language of children is more simple than that of adults when it may actually be more complex and more expressive. Children respond to colors, sounds, shapes, and gestures along with verbal behavior. Remember, children's feelings are very much like those of adults, but their thought processes are quite different.

Complimentary Tone

The tone of children's sermons is just as important as the verbal language selected to convey the message. Young children are not confident about verbal language. Therefore, they often center on the tone of the message. While the content of children's sermons may be lost on some children, they almost always "tune into" the tone of the message.

Tone is much more than just the delivery of the message. Tone conveys to the children valuable information about the speaker. Factors such as the presenter's physical presence (sitting or standing), dress, voice, and physical contact work together to create an atmosphere for children's sermons. The presenter should use the verbal message and tone to create an environment that is safe for children. Effective use of these verbal and nonverbal elements can give children a sense of security and the impression that their feelings are respected. If the verbal message and tone do not match, children receive conflicting messages and may actually ignore both.

Involvement of Senses

Communication with children, especially those aged 3-7, should involve as many of the senses as possible. Learning should take place in terms of events children can experience. The context of children's sermons within the sanctuary is a rich setting with a variety of sights, sounds, movements, and smells. And because of the difficulty involved with holding the attention of young children with voice alone, visual elements are important in effective children's sermons. The spoken word, however, is the usual method of conveying meaning.

Age-Appropriateness

The greatest challenge to communicating on the level of children is the wide discrepancy in the ages of the participants: 2-10 or older. For all practical purposes, it is impossible to prepare a sermon or homily for this age group that will be developmentally appropriate for each. Such a group would have three distinctly different developmental stages represented.

Two-year-olds are just beginning to feel comfortable with language, and their vocabulary and attention span are still quite limited. The younger ones are, to a great degree, still relating to their world through their senses and motoric behaviors. In contrast, 3-7 year-olds have functional vocabularies, excellent imaginations, love to play and imitate, are egocentric, believe that innate objects can be lifelike, have little notion of the concept of intent (rules are rules and cannot be broken under any circumstances), and think in illogical ways ("the stars are following us"). Even more distinctive, 8-11 year-olds consider several features of the same problem rather than focusing on only one aspect of it, can reverse thinking (back to the beginning of a problem), are able to consider how others feel, are fascinated with language and its different meanings, and are able to take into account the motives of others when judging their behaviors. But children this age are still limited in their thinking to their own experiences; they are limited to concrete, tangible problems.

This kind of age diversity in a Sunday morning children's sermon presentation presents a herculean challenge. One answer is to focus on the 2-7 year-olds one Sunday and the older children the next. Another solution is to offer something for each developmental level. The presentation can also stress the importance of being included in "big church" activities. Recent research reveals that presenters of children's sermons view the primary purpose of the sermon as inclusion in worship with the "big people." Perhaps in a situation with great age diversity, brevity, tone, and attitude are as important if not more so than what is actually said. Simply stated, the children hear what their developmental processes permit them to hear, and often what they perceive is not at all what the presenter intends.

Since children (and adults) perceive or interpret information based on their own experiences and at their developmental level, it is essential for the presenter to have some understanding of the way preschool and elementary school children think. Getting into the head of a 4-year-old, for instance, is usually difficult for adults.

Several years ago my wife, Mary, and I took our 4-year-old granddaughter, Mary Katherine, to a restaurant for dinner. Mary Katherine ordered chicken fingers with the experience of a seasoned gourmet. When the waitress brought her order, she brightened and said, "Papa, she knew I was 4 years old." I asked her how she knew, and she replied with confidence,

"Because there are 4 chicken fingers on my plate." There was no question in her mind. The waitress knew. To some, the answer may have appeared convoluted and even weird. But actually Mary Katherine was responding like a typical, bright, energetic 4-year-old. Her answer reflected her experiences and developmental level. She had been going to restaurants all her life, and she expressed verbal behavior that was illogical and egocentric.

Concreteness

The developmental stages of the children participating in children's sermons dictate that concreteness as opposed to generalness or abstractness is a necessary element of the sermons, regardless of the method used. Concreteness can be either tangible or intangible. While tangible concreteness may be a specific object, such as a puppet, costume, picture, or anything that can be seen and handled, intangible concreteness is expressed in terms of human experience and presence. These feelings and states include anger, fear, pride, selfishness, loneliness, kindness, compassion, and joy, and are familiar to children when placed into the experiences of their lives. Children's sermons that use a concrete object to represent abstract meanings are not always concrete in the way that is most helpful to children. Tangible props, therefore, should not be the sole focus of the sermon.

Simplicity

Elementary school-aged children have basic needs that should be considered when preparing to address them. Abraham Maslow provided insight into this subject by suggesting that basic needs such as food, water, shelter, safety, love, and esteem must be met before enrichment or growth needs such as knowledge, understanding, cultural enlightenment, and self-actualization are considered. Children's sermons should reflect a concern for both the basic and growth needs of children. Certainly the adult congregation should receive spiritual nourishment, but such a benediction should be a byproduct rather than the primary focus of the children's time.

Individuals are usually in their teens before they have the physical, cognitive, and social abilities necessary to sustain, comprehend, and appreciate all aspects of a worship service. Therefore, a 2-3 minute homily is developmentally appropriate for children's sermons. The sermon should make a central point connecting it to something in the children's experience and be illustrated in terms as simple as possible. If in doubt, choose simplicity. Even then the younger children (2-4 years old) will not always fully understand the point, but they will enjoy being included in the activities.

Sensitivity

One of the major temptations of presenters is to use children's sermons as an "entertainment break" in the worship hour. Too often, and sometimes unintentionally, presenters succumb to the desire to be "cute" with the children, to use them as "set-ups" for clever comments, as in the case of the presenter who asked the children how many of them had pets. He pointed to one little boy who said, "I have a cat," and then the child said something very softly to which the presenter responded loudly, "Your cat did *what* on the living room carpet?" The congregation roared, and the presenter looked quite pleased with himself. What was not noticed, however, was how the child reacted. Children often do not understand the difference in laughing with someone and being laughed at.

Eye-Level Contact

Effective communication with children also stresses eye-level contact. Children do indeed live in a "land of giants." They spend their childhoods looking up. It is prudent, therefore, to make every attempt to address the hearers at eye-level. Being at their level will enable the presenter to better "read" the verbal and nonverbal behaviors of the participants. Addressing the children at eye-level will also help avoid the tendency to "preach" to the "big people" rather than the "little people."

Routine

Repetition is a part of children's lives. It makes them feel secure and enables them to predict what is going to happen next. Children love viewing the same cartoons over and over, reading the same books again and again, and hearing the same stories repeatedly. It is, therefore, both appropriate and desirable to repeat Bible stories and other references in the presentation of children's sermons. Since sameness and routine are important to children, having the same presenter each Sunday is advisable.

Types of Sermons

Many of the guidelines for preparing children's sermons are based on the results of a survey conducted on their use in various denominations. Following is a summary of the research data. (Details of the survey are given in the third section of this book.)

- Children's sermons are part of the regular Sunday morning worship hour in a significant number of congregations in mainline Protestant denominations in the Bible Belt of the United States.

- 75% of the churches had memberships of 500 or less.

- There was an even distribution of churches responding among all geographic locations.

- More than 50% of the respondents indicated that the minister or associate minister presented the children's sermon.

- More than 50% of the respondents indicated that they had received some information about children's development from college, seminary, or graduate school.

- 79% of the respondents said they had completed at least one academic credit course in child development or related fields.

- More Presbyterian and United Methodist churches reported having children's sermons than those that reported not having a children's sermon.

- 1/3 of the churches reported that children begin attending the children's sermon at age 3, while almost 2/3 reported that 10 years or above is typically the age when children stop attending.

- Demonstration is the primary method of presentation of children's sermons, followed by storytelling and question and answer dialogue.

- Children's sermon presenters use material from Bible stories, literature illustrating biblical teachings, and personal experiences.

Children's sermons, like other sermons, may begin with the text and be based, when appropriate, upon the same Scripture as the regular sermon, thus developing a theme that continues throughout the entire service. A unified worship theme, however, can be detrimental to children's sermons when the theme is forced. Parenthetically, it is not necessary to read the biblical text; paraphrasing or story form is generally more appropriate. Presenters can also use the international church calendar and/or thematic series as organizational schemes for children's homilies. The key to a successful children's sermon, however, is to catch and hold children's imaginative participation in the subject chosen. The presentation methodology selected is paramount. There are, according to research, three primary methodologies utilized in presenting children's sermons: object lessons, stories, and dialogue.

Object Lessons

Object lessons, a popular form of children's sermons, are most often metaphorical. The understanding of metaphor is directly related to mental development. Metaphorical language often confuses children who think literally. Another form of object lessons, however, is the use of an object as a visual aid to hold the children's attention and provide an introduction to a moral lesson. Object lessons have the advantage of combining the oral-aural with the visual. Some writers believe the best form is the creative use of objects in well-planned and structured lessons that respect the integrity of the children. Not everyone agrees, however. Some believe that object lessons are more appropriate for youth and adults. In fact, adults enjoy them over other forms of children's sermons.

The dangers of object lessons are numerous. Object lessons often fail to take into account how children learn and think. Most object lessons require children to conserve, which is a cognitive process many children have not yet mastered. Conservation requires an individual to understand the concept characteristics of an object and to transfer this information to an abstract concept. In object lessons the children are required to transfer their concrete understanding to a moral lesson or a biblical truth. The use of words and phrases such as "stands for," "relates to," and "like," demand a shift in thinking (conservation) that is inappropriate for young children. For instance, the following statements can completely confuse young children: "Life is like a baseball game. You win some; you lose some." "When a tadpole becomes a frog, something new emerges, and that relates to what happens when we become Christians—we are new beings."

Too often object lessons are not effective because presenters have a tendency to moralize and abstract when delivering the message. Object lessons also have a tendency to become abstract when attention is centered on the object rather than on the message the object illustrates. Another problem with object lessons is the reliance on external objects. Objects can distract the children's attention away from the point of the sermon. As a result, the children only remember the object(s) and not the explanation. In view of the risks in object lessons, their use may require more discipline and preparation than other forms of children's sermons.

Stories

Children respond well to episode, and narrative in particular. Therefore, stories in varied forms and styles are preferred for children's sermons. They can be combined with other forms to foster effective communication with children. Stories in the context of worship are oral-aural events, and when visual aids and other sensory experiences are employed, their effectiveness is maximized. The content should, of course, be directed to the children's current developmental stage or stages.

A key to developing faith for preschool children and preparing a framework for later faith is based on the development of children's imaginative capacities and a foundational order in reality in which children can trust. Stories such as fantasies and fables that involve the fears, anxieties, and joys of children should be set in a context where good triumphs over evil. These stories stimulate childhood imagination and give meaning to the rituals and order of the faith community. Many of these myths and narratives are later reviewed and evaluated by the participants when they reach another level of cognitive processing.

The person responsible for conducting children's sermons must be able to function as a practical theologian, someone who is clear about the basic principles of the Christian faith. In general, the most important content of teaching for preschoolers are the stories of the Bible. Scripture lends itself to the forms of teaching that are appropriate for children in this stage. Bible stories can provide children with a foundation on which they can begin to build their own image of God. Because young children live in a world of imagination and fantasy, they are not surprised by miracles. They do not recognize the irregularity and illogic of the miracle, however. Too much emphasis upon the miracle stories may reinforce the idea that God and Superman are brothers.

Stories continue to stimulate the imagination of literal-minded children. These stories also provide children with the basic knowledge of human life upon which faith builds in later life. The development of stories for children's sermons should draw heavily on the imaginative, reflective, and affective. The retelling of Bible stories is always appropriate. Bible stories give children a feel for the language of the Christian community and at the same time communicate in a language children understand.

For children in the literal early childhood stage, the world of fantasy still exists, but they also have a growing sense of concrete reality. Narratives should involve stories of heroes and heroines that can help to develop the imagination and provide models for individual achievement and the development of community that emerges in the next stage. Children's understanding of symbols is literalistic. While stories and myth have tremendous influence over the imagination and organize the world for children, stories are interpreted literally and are limited to the concrete experiences of children.

Another story strategy that can be helpful is incorporating "when I was a little boy/girl" stories. Our two oldest grandchildren, David and Daniel, constantly request stories about "when Papa was a little boy." Sometimes the requests are very specific, for example: "Papa, tell us about the time you went to the Big Ditch and found those crawfish" or "Tell us about when you planted the garden with your granddaddy." Again, children love to hear stories they have heard before. Such stories help them feel safe, secure, and involved.

Dialogue

Children's sermons based on question and answer dialogue between the presenter and children are not predominant forms. Although sermons of this nature are appealing, they can be tricky. This dualism may be the reason for the apparent lack of interest in this methodology.

A dialogue between presenter and children is an informal children's sermon. The children's contributions are welcomed and respected. The challenging part of this type of children's sermon is the unpredictable nature of children. The questions asked of the children should capture the children's interest and be open-ended. Asking good questions means the presenter must be sensitive to the children's experiences and thinking. When using the question and answer methodology, the presenter must be ready to field all kinds of responses without turning the questions and/or the answers into entertainment for the congregation. The dialogue method has the advantage of involvement for the children and can make the participants feel important and valued.

Practical Considerations

Regardless of the methodology employed, a summary of the previous week's homily is needed at the beginning of a new children's sermon and an announcement of the next week's topic should follow the current presentation. Certainly these two suggestions are not always fitting, but attention to the ideas may be useful.

It is not always appropriate to give children a gift at the end of children's sermons, but it is certainly timely to do so on many occasions. The gift can be a part of an object lesson or can be related or unrelated to the topic of the day. It would be better to give a present intermittently than to give one on a continuous schedule. Children do not need to expect a gift each time they attend, but a present on an occasional basis is acceptable.

When all is thought, prepared, and presented, the primary purposes of children's sermons are to include the children in authentic worship experiences and to create an awareness and sensitivity to the customs, rituals, routines, vocabulary, and intentions of the congregation. Method of presentation will vary, and time and content of the homilies will change from Sunday to Sunday, but the church's dedication to "the least of these" should remain.

In the next section of the book there are 60 homilies prepared with sensitivity to the various age groups and developmental levels that may be present for children's sermons. The 40 sermons of a general nature are more appropriate for children ages 3-6, and the 13 sermons that explain "church words" and the 7 special days presentations are fitting for use with children age 7 or above. With changes in vocabulary and illustrations, however, developmentally appropriate adaptations can be made. For example, if some or all of the children are older than 7 or 8, the presenter may want to add some complexity to the contents, change some of the vocabulary, and add or subtract material. If the participants are ages 2-5, the presenter may want to simplify the contents and vocabulary. A mixed-age group, for example, ages 2-10, presents the greatest communication challenge.

Another option is to omit the summary of the previous week's sermon and/or the announcement of the next week's topic. The sermons may be presented as dialogues, object lessons, stories, or a combination of these methods. A dialogue can be turned into a lecture/story by omitting the questions or phrasing questions in a rhetorical manner. The materials recommended for some of the homilies are, of course, optional. Remember, adaptability to a unique situation is the key to usability.

The following is a summary of preparation suggestions offered in this section. Frequent review of these guidelines should prove beneficial, especially to persons who work with children on a limited basis.

- Concentrate on the needs of the children, not on the congregational entertainment value of the presentation.

- Children perceive, or interpret, on the basis of their experiences, which are, of course, limited in contrast to those of adults.

- Children like repetition. Therefore, do not hesitate to repeat stories, biblical references, and materials.

- A short homily of 2 or 3 minutes that contains a central point is preferred over a longer, multiple message presentation.

- Keep words simple and within the experiences of the children.

- Meet children at their eye level. Do not stand or tower over them.

- Sameness and routine are important to children. Therefore, if possible, have the same person present the children's sermon each Sunday.

- When appropriate, try to coordinate the children's sermon with the sermon of the morning, but do not force the coordination.

- Involve the children as much as feasible in the homily.

- Do not turn children's responses to your questions into jokes for the congregation.

- Children often do not understand the difference between laughing with someone and being laughed at.

- At the beginning of the homily, summarize the previous week's sermon.

- At the end of the homily, give the children an idea of what will be discussed the following week.

- Always talk to and with children, not the congregation.

- When appropriate, give the participants something related to the topic (such as a flower, a rock, or a Band-Aid) to take with them.

- Remember that the theme of the sermon for children should be to create an awareness and sensitivity to the customs, rituals, routines, vocabulary, and overall purpose of the congregation and to help the children feel included in the worship experience.

- Children like to hear "when I was a little boy/girl" stories.

- When you ask questions, be ready to field all kinds of responses without turning the answer into entertainment for the congregation.

- Do not feel that your children's sermons are too simplistic. They will be for you and your adult congregation, but they will not be for preschool and early elementary-age children.

- If in doubt about word usage in your presentation, choose the more simple word or term.

- Involve as many of the five senses as possible.

- Connect the main idea in the sermon to common experiences of the children.

- Children's feelings are much like those of adults, but their thought processes are quite different from those of adults.

Model Children's Sermons

General Topics

God Loves Everybody
John 3:16

Materials: a picture showing different kinds of people for each child

Today we will talk about the kinds of people God loves. People do all sorts of things in God's world. People help other people. And some people hurt other people.

The newspapers, television, our parents, and our teachers tell us about both the good things and the bad things people do. For example, I recently read about a man who gave a lot of money to a college so big kids could go there free. That was a very nice gift!

I also read about a person who hurt his children and would not let them go to school or church. He was a very mean man and did bad things to his family. God did not like what this man did.

God, does, however, love both the good man and the bad man. God loves all boys and girls, teenagers, and adults. When you are bad and disobey your parents, they tell you they are disappointed in you, and they may even punish you, but they still love you very much. God is like that, too. God does not approve of our being bad, but God always loves us.

Thank you, God, for loving all of us. Amen.

Notes

· ·

· ·

· ·

· ·

Healthy Bodies

Leviticus 19:28; 1 Corinthians 3:16; Psalms 139:14

Last week we talked about how much God loves us. Today we will talk about keeping our bodies healthy.

How many of you have been to the doctor lately? What did the doctor do? (Wait for responses.) She probably looked in your ears and your eyes and your mouth. You may have gotten a shot, too. And she listened to your heart.

How about the dentist? How many of you have seen your dentist in the last few weeks? What did he do? (Wait for responses.) I'll bet your dentist looked at your teeth and maybe even filled a cavity.

Doctors and dentists help us keep our bodies healthy. But we have to help ourselves. What can we do to keep our bodies from being sick? (Wait for responses.) Yes, we need to take baths regularly, eat good food, drink lots of water, wear warm clothing in winter and keep cool in summer, brush our teeth, and get lots of sleep. God is pleased when we keep our bodies well.

Next week we will talk about getting mad or anger.

Lord, help us to keep our bodies well. Amen.

Notes

. . . .

. . . .

. . . .

. . . .

Anger
Matthew 5:22; Exodus 32:ff

What did we talk about last week? (Wait for responses.) Good. Today we will discuss anger, getting mad. How many of you have gotten angry or mad? What was it about? (Wait for responses.)

We get mad about lots of things, don't we? When someone pushes us down or takes the toy we are playing with, or if mom or dad won't let us go next door to play, we may get angry or mad about it.

The Bible has lots of stories about people who got angry. Moses got very angry with the people he was preaching to and threw down some important books and damaged them. It was alright for him to be angry because the people he preached to had been very bad, but he should not have damaged the books.

Getting mad or angry is normal, but staying mad and hitting people and being ugly just because we don't get what we want is not good. God understands when we get mad, but God does not want us to stay mad or to hurt ourselves or others when we are angry.

Next week we will talk about the environment.

God, help us to control our anger. Amen.

Notes

. . . .

. . . .

. . . .

. . . .

The Environment
Genesis 1:31

Materials: a piece of fruit for each child

This week we will talk about a big, big subject: the environment. What in the world is the environment? (Wait for responses.) Good. The environment is everything that is around us: the air we breathe, the water we drink, the land that grows our food, the forests that provide wood for us, the animals that live in the forests and on the land, and people like us who also live on this earth.

The Bible says that God made the earth and the animals and the people. After God made all of the earth, animals, and people, He looked everything over and said He was pleased.

Everything in God's world has a purpose, and everything God made works together. For example, you may see a dead tree in your backyard or in a park and say, "That old tree is not doing any good." But look again. You may see holes in the tree where birds and other creatures live, and you may see birds hunting for bugs (food) in that tree. What is this? (Hold up a piece of fruit.) Right. This is an apple. After I eat this apple, I can put the core, or what is left, in the ground, and it will decay and become part of the soil.

Perhaps you have seen your parents put potato peelings, apple and orange peelings, and parts of vegetables in a bowl and carry them to the yard to bury them. They are putting some of what came from the earth back into the earth where it will rot and become a part of the soil. At your school you may have places to place soda and juice cans. When you put your cans in those containers, you are helping the environment. You are recycling.

Remember, all of God's creation has a purpose. One of our purposes is to protect and take care of God's world.

God, thank you for making our world. Help us to take good care of it. Amen.

Notes

. . . .

. . . .

Taking a Field Trip

Genesis 1:31

Materials: a toy car or bus for each child

Last week we learned about taking care of the environment. Today we will talk about taking a field trip.

What is a field trip? (Wait for responses; prompting may be needed.) Well done. A field trip is when we leave where we are and go somewhere else and learn something new. Schoolchildren often take field trips to places such as zoos, parks, and museums. When they return to their classrooms, they talk about what they saw and did. They may name the animals they saw at the zoo such as lions, tigers, snakes, monkeys, elephants, and giraffes. They probably talk about the equipment they played on in the park—slides, merry-go-rounds, swings, and tree houses. Museums are fun field trips, too. You can see pictures of famous people and old things such as tractors and cars and trains and houses.

You know, coming to church is kind of like a field trip. You leave home and come here and learn something new every time you come. Then when you go home, you can talk to your family about what you learned. Maybe when you go home today, you can talk to your family about the kind of field trips you would like to go on.

Next week we will talk about a boy and a giant!

Thank you, God, that we can go to different places and see your wonderful creations. Amen.

Notes

. . . .

. . . .

. . . .

. . . .

A Boy and a Giant
1 Samuel 17:49

Materials: slingshot

This week we will talk about a boy and also a man who was very big, a giant! The Bible tells a story about a boy named David who helped his dad tend their sheep. He worked very hard keeping up with their sheep. One day he heard that a very large man was being mean to his friends and that his friends could not get the huge man to leave them alone.

So David left the sheep on the hillside and went to where Goliath the giant was bothering his friends. Many of the grownups had tried to run the giant off, but they had not succeeded. David told his friends that he could get rid of the big man for them. They asked him where his sword was, but David just showed them his slingshot. His friends laughed and said he could not do much with that slingshot. But David said he had used that slingshot to kill lions that had tried to eat his father's sheep. Finally they let David, the boy, face Goliath, the giant. David put a stone in the slingshot and threw the stone at the giant and killed him. His friends were so happy that the giant was dead and they were safe again.

Like David, no matter how small we are, we can always try to help. Even when a job looks too big for us, like washing a big car by ourselves, we can help. And when we get a little older, we can do big jobs by ourselves.

Thank you, God, for stories like the one about David and the giant. Amen.

Notes

· ·

· ·

· ·

· ·

Pleasing God
Ephesians 5:10

Last week we talked about David and Goliath. This week our subject is doing what pleases God. This is a hard subject to understand, isn't it? The Bible speaks of doing what is acceptable to God, which means doing what pleases God.

Since we cannot see God or reach out and touch God, it is hard to know what God wants us to do. But there are some ways we can discover what pleases God. One way is to come to Sunday School and church and listen to the minister and to our other church teachers as they explain what the stories in the Bible mean. Another way we can know what pleases God is to ask our moms and dads to read (or you read) stories from the Bible to us. And then we can talk about them. One of the best ways to know what pleases God is to watch people who believe in God and obey God's rules. Ask your parents to help you find these people.

Next week we will discuss babies.

Lord, help us to do what pleases you. Amen.

Notes

. . . .

. . . .

. . . .

. . . .

Babies
Proverbs 22:6

Today we will talk about babies. Do any of you have a baby at your house? (Wait for responses.) What do babies do? (Wait for responses.) Right. They cry, eat, mess in their diapers, drink milk, and sleep a lot. When they get a little older, they smile, sit up, crawl, walk, and get into your toys! Holding babies is fun, isn't it. And watching them grow and learn new things is fun, too. But taking care of babies is a big job, right? How many of you help take care of your baby sister or brother? (Wait for responses.) Great!

Remember when you were smaller? Mom and dad had to feed you, dress you, and watch over you very carefully. All of us have been babies, and it makes us feel good to remember that our parents took good care of us when we were not big enough to feed ourselves, or walk, or dress ourselves, or go to the bathroom alone.

Thinking about being babies makes us feel warm and cozy. And sometimes when we have lots to do, we may want to be a baby again! But we have to keep growing and learning new things. But even as we get older, it is nice to know that mom and dad still take care of us and keep us safe and bring us to church.

Lord, thank you for our parents who keep us safe. Amen.

Notes

. . . .

. . . .

. . . .

. . . .

Sleeping at the Wrong Time
Acts 20:9ff

Last week in our time together we discussed babies. This week we will talk about a boy in the Bible who went to sleep at the wrong time. His name was Eutychus, and he had gone to church to hear a man named Paul preach. He must not have been able to find a seat in church, so he climbed up and sat in a window.

Eutychus must have had a good view, but he made a big mistake. He went to sleep and fell out the window and hurt himself. But after a while he got well. This boy was a little like Humpty-Dumpy. Remember him? He sat on a wall, maybe went to sleep, and fell off the wall. The nursery rhyme says that he was hurt so badly, he could not be put together again.

What we learn from these stories is that there are times when we need to pay attention and not go to sleep. We need to pay attention when our parents and our teachers talk to us. We also should pay attention when we are playing with our friends, when we cross the street, and when we do our homework.

Next week our topic for the children's sermon will be rules.

Oh God, help us to pay attention when we need to. Amen.

Notes

· ·

· ·

· ·

· ·

Rules
Exodus 20:1ff

Materials: a ruler for each child

What was last week's sermon about? (Wait for responses; prompting may be necessary). Good! This week we will talk about rules. What is this? (Hold up ruler; wait for responses.) Excellent. It is a ruler, and we use rulers to measure things. For example, a ruler tells us how tall we are in feet and inches.

Rules tell us what to do, and hearing the rule over and over tells us how well we are doing in obeying the rule.

God has given us rules to live by. These rules in the Bible are called commandments. By reading these rules, we know what to do, and we know if we are failing to "measure up" to God's rule. For example, one of God's rules is to obey our parents. Have you heard of that rule before? (Wait for responses.) What can we do to obey our parents? We can listen to what they say to us and do what they tell us, can't we?

Lord, help us to obey your rules. Amen.

Notes

. . . .

. . . .

. . . .

. . . .

Love Your Friends, and Love Yourself
Romans 13:9

Materials: a mirror

Today we will talk about how important it is not only to like or love our neighbors or friends, but also like or love ourselves. (Show children the mirror) Who do you see? (Wait for responses.) Yes, you!

What does it mean to like or love yourself? (Wait for responses; prompting may be needed) Good. Loving ourselves means that we think well of ourselves, that we believe in ourselves. For example, when someone asks us to read, if we can't read, it's okay to say, "I can't read yet, but I'm learning." Or when we are asked to help clean up the yard, we can say, "Sure, I can do that, and I will do my best." With those kind of answers we are saying "there arc some things I can do and some things I can't do yet, but I can learn." We are saying that we believe in ourselves.

Remember, God believes in us and knows that we are good boys and girls who can do many things.

Help us, Oh God, to believe in you and in ourselves. Amen.

Notes

. . . .

. . . .

. . . .

. . . .

Loving Your Enemies
Genesis 37:1ff; Luke 6:27

Today we will talk about a boy in the Bible named Joseph. Joseph's family was large. He had several brothers and sisters who were older than he. Joseph's brothers were very jealous of him. They thought their father paid too much attention to Joseph. He bought special presents for Joseph, things like expensive toys and clothes.

Joseph's brothers got so mad at Joseph that they tried to get rid of him. They took him way out in the country and for awhile left him in a hole in the ground. But then they decided to sell him to some people who lived far away.

Joseph grew up to be a very important man in his new country. Many years passed, and Joseph's father and family became hungry because there was little food in their country. When Joseph found out that his family was hungry, he gave them food from his country. Joseph could have been angry with his brothers because they took him away from his father and his home and sold him into slavery. But Joseph returned love to his brothers rather than staying mad with them. He fed them instead of trying to get even by starving them.

Lord, help us to learn to return good for bad. Amen.

Notes

. . . .

. . . .

. . . .

. . . .

Light for the Darkness
Psalms 119:105

Materials: flashlight

What did we talk about last week? (Wait for responses.) Good! Today we will talk about this (hold up flashlight). What is it? (Wait for responses.) That's right, a flashlight. What do we use flashlights for? (Wait for responses.) True. Flashlights help us see where we are going when it is dark. It's good to have something that shines in the dark to show us the way, isn't it.

Flashlights are not the only things that help us find our way when it is dark or when we are lost. I remember when I was a little boy and would be going somewhere with my mom or dad, and it would get dark. I would hold my mom or dad's hand, and they would know right where they were going.

Sometimes our parents and teachers ask us to do something, but we don't know how to do it, so we ask them for help. Not knowing what to do or the answer to a question is kind of like being in the dark without a flashlight. But when our parents and teachers help us, they are like flashlights shining light in the dark. They help us find our way when we are lost or when we don't know something.

Next week we will talk about rules.

Thank you, God, for parents and teachers who help us know answers to questions. Amen.

Notes

. . . .

. . . .

. . . .

. . . .

Another of God's Rules

Exodus 20:15

Materials: a ballpoint pen for each child

Last week we talked about light for the darkness. Several weeks ago we talked about God's rules being called commandments. We specifically discussed God's rule that we were to obey our parents. Remember?

Well, today we will talk about another of God's rules. This rule says we are not to steal. What does steal mean? (Wait for responses.) That's very good. It means we are not to take anything that does not belong to us.

(Hold up the ballpoint pen.) What is this? (Wait for responses.) Right. It is a pen. There are several ways I could have gotten this pen. I could have bought it. I could have borrowed it from a friend. I could have found it on the floor of the classroom, or I could have stolen it. But stealing it would be wrong, not honest, against God's rule. And if I had found it at school, I should take it to the teacher so she could find out who had lost it. If I had borrowed the pen, I should return it. Actually, I bought this pen—which is the way many of us get our pens.

Oh God, help us to be honest in all we do. Amen.

Notes

. . . .

. . . .

. . . .

. . . .

What Pictures Tell Us
Matthew 21:1ff

Materials: photographs of yourself at different developmental stages

Today we will talk about photographs or pictures. Who do you think this is? (Wait for responses.) Hey guys. That's me as a baby! What about this one? (Wait for responses.) Very good. That's me as a teenager. And this one? (Wait for responses.) You got it! That's my church directory picture.

I'll bet your parents have lots of pictures of you. Right? When you get older, you will look at these photographs and know what you looked like years before. Books such as the Bible give us word pictures of how people lived hundreds of years ago, what they did for a living and how they behaved. For example, the Bible tells us stories about Jesus and how he worked in his dad's workshop when he was a boy and what he did when he went to church.

We don't have any photographs of Jesus, but we do have stories in the Bible about him, and we can use our imagination when we read or hear stories about him working with his dad or going to church or later when he was an adult preaching to people.

Thank you, God, for pictures and words that tell us about people. Amen.

Notes

. . . .

. . . .

. . . .

. . . .

Making Good Use of a Pencil

Matthew 18:27

Materials: a pencil with an eraser for each child

Today we will talk about this (hold up the pencil). What is it? (Wait for responses.) That's right! It is a pencil. What do you do with it? (Wait for responses.) Excellent. You print with it, write with it, and draw with it. It is very useful, isn't it.

We need pencils for our work and play in school and at home. What is your favorite thing to do with a pencil? Great! Draw, print, and write. What happens when you print, write, or draw something and you make a mistake? (Wait for responses.) That's right. You use the eraser on the other end of the pencil and start over.

Erasers are really neat, aren't they? Erasers allow us to wipe out the mistake and start over. That's what happens when we make a mistake at home and ask mom and dad to forgive us. They say "yes," and we get to start over. Forgiveness is like an eraser. Our parents forgive us when we are bad or do something wrong, and we get to start over. God forgives us, too, when we ask Him for forgiveness. We get to start over.

Thank you, God, for allowing us to start over. Amen.

Notes

. . . .

. . . .

. . . .

. . . .

Being a Friend
Proverbs 18:24

Last week we talked about pencils and erasers. Today we will talk about friends. What is a friend? (Wait for responses.) Good. A friend is someone we like to play with or talk to or watch TV with.

Sometimes when our friends come to see us or we go to their houses, they want to play one game, but we don't want to play that game. A real friend will do what their friends want to do—if it's the right thing to do, at least for awhile. And then you can change games and play what you want to play. It is good to have that kind of friend.

Some children have lots of friends, which is nice. But it's really sad to see children who do not have friends. Perhaps this week you can try to be a friend to someone who does not have a friend. God likes for us to have friends and to be a friend.

Next week we will talk about love.

God, help us to be good friends. Amen.

Notes

. . . .

. . . .

. . . .

. . . .

How Old Is Love?

1 John 4:7

This week we will talk about the oldest thing in the world. Do you know what it is? (Wait for responses.) No, it's not a dog, a rock, a mountain, a tree, a bird, or a flower. It is not even the old man named Methuselah who the Bible says lived 969 years. That's almost 1,000 years! The Bible is not even the oldest thing in the world. What about shoes? Are they the oldest thing in the world? No. How about cars? No. Okay. What about milk? Nope! That's not it either.

I'll bet I have it: water. Water is the oldest thing in the world. What do you think? (Wait for responses.) I think I fooled you. No, it's not water or light or darkness or lions or tigers.

The oldest thing in the world is love. God loved so much that He made the world and all things in it. Mom and dad love you with that kind of love. And this church family loves each one of you, too.

Thank you, God, for loving us always. Amen.

Notes

. . . .

. . . .

. . . .

. . . .

Little Things Mean a Lot
Zechariah 4:10

Materials: the inside of a watch or a clock *or* a picture of small items such as screws, pins, nails, etc.

Last week's sermon was about love. Today we will talk about little things and how important they are. What is this? (Wait for responses.) That's right. It is the inside of a watch. Look at how many tiny screws and pieces are in this small circle-shaped container. If any one of these pieces is missing, the watch will not work.

Do you remember the nursery rhyme about how important a horseshoe nail is? The nail held the horseshoe on the horse. When the nail was lost, the horse could not carry the man who wanted to ride on him. And the man who wanted to ride on the horse was supposed to fight in a battle, but he could not go—all because the horseshoe nail was lost!

We need to remember that little things like screws for watches and nails for horseshoes are very important. For example, when we are given a job to do, no matter how little it seems, we need to do it. If mom tells us to take out the garbage and we don't, guess what? After a while that garbage may start smelling really bad. So what may have seemed like a little job was really, really important. God believes all of our work is important.

Next week we will talk about how to learn about God.

Lord, help us to see how important little things are. Amen.

Notes

. . . .

. . . .

. . . .

. . . .

How Do We Learn about God?

Romans 10:1-4

Today we will talk about how we learn about God. How do you think you learn about God? (Wait for responses.) Very good.

We learn about God by going to church, taking part in the children's sermon, and going to Sunday School. We also learn about God from our parents who read us stories about God and teach us to pray. We learn about God from the Bible, a book that has many interesting stories: stories about animals, farmers, and families; stories about good people and bad people; stories about fishing and about Jesus. We also learn about God from our friends. One of the best ways we learn about God is by singing songs about God. Let's all sing "Jesus Loves Me."

God, help us to learn more about you. Amen.

Notes

. . . .

. . . .

. . . .

. . . .

Teamwork
Philippians 1:27

Materials: a picture of a group of people or animals working together for each child

This week we will talk about teamwork, or working together. Have any of you guys played on a team? (Wait for responses.) Which teams have you played on? (Wait for responses.) Very good.

There are all kinds of teams, aren't there? When we hear the word team, we often think of sports teams—like basketball, soccer, football, and baseball. There are also teams that involve animals. I was watching the Discovery Channel the other day and saw eight or ten beautiful dogs pulling a sled. The dogs were working together to pull that sled and the person standing on the sled.

That's the purpose of a team, isn't it? To work together to accomplish something. Sometimes our teachers ask a few of us to work together on a project. Sometimes mom and dad ask us as a family to be a team and work together to do jobs such as clean the yard.

The Bible tells stories about teamwork. Jesus and his friends, called disciples, worked together to help people and tell them about God.

Lord, help us to work together to help people in your name. Amen.

Notes

. . . .

. . . .

. . . .

. . . .

Butterflies Are Beautiful

Psalm 50:1-2; Ecclesiastes 3:11

Materials: butterfly net, butterfly (dead or in a jar), and a picture of a butterfly for each child

This week we will talk about butterflies. (Hold up the butterfly net and butterfly in turn.) What is this? (Wait for responses.) Right, a butterfly net. And what is this? (Wait for responses.) Very good, a butterfly.

Butterflies are among God's most interesting and beautiful creatures. It takes a while for a butterfly to get ready to come into the world. When the butterfly begins to fly, he helps make God's world beautiful. Butterflies are very gentle creatures. Sometimes they will even land on your hand or your shoulder or your nose!

God makes different kinds of butterflies—white ones, black ones, brown ones, red ones, yellow ones, and all mixed-up colors ones—just like people. God made people in different colors and all sizes. Butterflies, too, come in all sizes—tiny, medium, and large.

Isn't God's world a wonderful place of beauty?

Thank you, God, for the beauty of your world. Amen.

Notes

. . . .

. . . .

. . . .

. . . .

Giving
2 Corinthians 9:11

Materials: an offering plate; a small bank for each child

Today we will talk about this (hold offering plate for children to see). What is it? Excellent. It is a plate used to collect offerings of money given by people in our church.

How do you give your money offering to church or Sunday School? (Wait for responses.) Very good! The Bible has many stories about people who gave offerings to God. Do you remember the stories about the poor lady who gave all the money she had to Jesus and the little boy who gave his lunch of fish and bread to Jesus?

What are some ways we can give to our church? (Wait for responses; prompting may be needed.) Yes, we can give our money, and we can give canned goods or food on special days to help feed hungry people. We can give clothes to the church "clothes closet" to help people who need clothes. We can also collect toys for needy children at Christmas. God is happy when we give to our church.

God, help us to enjoy giving to our church. Amen.

Notes

. . . .

. . . .

. . . .

. . . .

Keeping Promises
Judges 16:4ff

This week we will talk about Samson, a man whose story is told in the Bible. Samson was a big strong man who promised to love God and work for him. He also had a secret with God.

God told Samson that as long as he did not cut his hair, he would be very strong and no one could beat him in a fight. But there were bad people who wanted to beat up Samson, and they wanted to know what the secret was that made him so strong.

Samson promised God he would keep his hair long and would not tell anyone that his strength came from his long hair. But Samson lied to God and told a friend about the secret. When Samson went to sleep, a man cut his hair. He was no longer strong.

The mean people beat up Samson and hurt him badly, but Samson learned his lesson. When his hair grew out, he kept his promise to God and won the battle with the bad people.

What have we learned from this story about Samson? (Wait for responses.) That's right. We should keep our promises, shouldn't we?

God, help us to keep our promises. Amen.

Notes

· ·

· ·

· ·

· ·

Being a Good Friend
1 Thessalonians 5:11

Today we will talk about two men in the Bible, Paul and Barnabas. Paul was a preacher. He talked to people about God. He went to a lot of churches. Sometimes what he preached made people mad. He told them they should love God and love each other and quit doing bad things. But some of the people did not want to hear that they should be good, and they said ugly things to Paul.

Sometimes Paul felt very sad and believed that all the people were against him. But Paul had a good friend named Barnabas. Barnabas would go see his friend Paul and cheer him up or encourage him. This made Paul feel better.

Wasn't it great that Paul had a friend who came to him when he needed him and who always tried to make him feel better? Let's try to be a friend like Barnabas and help our friends be better and feel better.

God, help us to be good friends and to be good at making people feel better. Amen.

Notes

. . . .

. . . .

. . . .

. . . .

The Lost Sheep and the Good Shepherd
John 10:14

Today we will talk about a farmer who had 100 sheep. That's a lot of animals to keep up with. But this farmer counted his sheep every night. One night when he counted, one sheep was missing.

The sheep farmer, or shepherd, began to look for the lost sheep. He called for the lost lamb and looked all over the field and in the valley and on the hillsides. Finally, he found the sheep tangled up in some vines. The lamb had been hurt, and the farmer picked her up and returned her to the barnyard with the other sheep.

The shepherd was good to his sheep. He loved each one of them and missed them when he was away from them or when one of them got away from the barn. The Bible says that Jesus is like that farmer. He loves us like the shepherd loved his sheep, and he misses us when we are away from him.

Thank you, God, for loving us and for wanting to look after us. Amen.

Notes

. . . .

. . . .

. . . .

. . . .

The Magic of Music
Psalm 150; Psalm 108:3

Materials: a musical instrument; a picture of a musical instrument or piece of music for each child

What did we talk about last week? (Wait for responses.) Today we will talk about music. What is this? (Hold up a musical instrument; wait for responses.) That's right. This is a _____. You put it to your mouth and blow, and out comes music. It's almost like magic, isn't it?

The Bible tells us about a man who was a king, but he also loved music and wrote music. This man's name was David. David wrote songs called "psalms." People used the psalms to help them worship God.

In our church we sing songs, and they help us say "thank you" to God for this wonderful world, our parents, our home, our friends, and our church. What are some of your favorite church songs? (Wait for responses.) Very good. Maybe you can remember to sing some of your favorite church songs this week. Why don't we sing a song now? Let's all sing together "Jesus Loves Me."

Next week we will talk about a box where we can put our complaints or gripes.

Thank you, God, for music. Amen.

Notes

· ·

· ·

· ·

· ·

The Complaint Box
Philippians 2:14

Material: a shoebox

Today we will talk about complaining. What does that big word mean? (Wait for responses.) Good. Complaining means griping, grumbling, or fussing. How many of you have griped or fussed about something in the last few days. (Wait for responses.) What did you fuss about? (Wait for responses.)

Your parents probably wanted you to pick up your toys, or be nice to your sister or brother, or be on time for Sunday School, or get fresh water for the cat, or get dressed for school. Right? And if you did not want to do those things, you complained or griped or fussed about having to do them. If we are not careful, we can develop a habit of complaining or fussing about almost everything. The weather is too hot, too cold, or too rainy. Our food is not our favorite. Our friends aren't nice to us or don't want to play what we want to play. A family member is mean to us.

I once read about a family that decided to do something about their complaining and fussing. (Hold up the shoebox.) The family members agreed that every time someone in the family complained, griped, grumbled, or fussed, they would have to put a penny in the "complaint box." At the end of every week the pennies were counted and given to the church. What about that idea? (Wait for responses.)

The Bible says we should do our jobs without complaining.

God, help us to do our jobs without fussing about them. Amen.

Notes

. . . .

. . . .

. . . .

Who Is Your Neighbor?
Luke 10:30ff

What was our children's sermon about last week? (Wait for responses.) Good. Today I want to share a Bible story with you. It is about being a good neighbor. What is a neighbor? (Wait for responses.) That's right. We usually think of neighbors as people who live close to us. But Jesus had a different idea of who a neighbor is.

Jesus told a story about a man who was taking a trip. Some bad people robbed him and beat him up and left him on the side of the road. After several people refused to help the man, one person saw him and rushed to give him help. Jesus said that the man who helped did not even know the man who had been robbed and beaten.

The point of this story is that our neighbor is anyone nearby who needs help. For example, when we see a child crying on the playground, we can ask her if we can help. Or if someone has both arms full, even though we may not know him, we can hold the door open for him. In doing so, we are being good neighbors.

Next week we will talk about sharing.

Oh God, help us to be good neighbors. Amen.

Notes

· ·

· ·

· ·

· ·

Sharing
John 6:9

Materials: a fishing pole or rod; two "goldfish" crackers for each child

This week we are going fishing—well, not really fishing, but we will talk about a little boy who did.

One day Jesus was talking to a large group of people. When lunchtime came, he wanted to give his friends something to eat, but he did not have anything with him. But there was a little boy there who had just caught two fish. He also had some bread.

The little boy gave his fish and bread to Jesus who shared them with his friends. This little boy could have been selfish and kept his lunch to himself, but he wanted to share. I'll bet the boy really felt good about helping feed his friends.

Jesus wants us to share with others, and we can learn to feel good that we have helped others. You know, I have a goldfish cracker. In fact, I have some extras in my pocket. I want to share with you. (Give each child two crackers, and urge them to share with someone else).

Lord, help us to learn to share with those who need help. Amen.

Notes

. . . .

. . . .

. . . .

. . . .

What Is God Like?

John 4:24

Materials: paper and a pencil for each child

Remember what we talked about last week? (Wait for responses.) Good. This week we will talk about what God is like. What do you think God is like? (Wait for responses.) That's right. God is caring. God is love. God is kind. God is forgiving. God is fair. God is in so many ways like our parents: loving, kind, forgiving, and caring.

I want each of you to take a piece of paper and a pencil. Draw a picture of what you think God looks like. We don't really know what God looks like because no one has seen God, so your drawing will be your very own idea.

(Wait a few seconds) Okay, what do you have? (Have children share their drawings.) Good job. You know, God looks a little like you. Take the paper and pencil with you and work on your picture later. Be sure and show it to your family when you finish.

Thank you, God, for loving and caring for us. Amen.

Notes

. . . .

. . . .

. . . .

. . . .

Windows
Luke 21:1-4

This week we will talk about windows. Do you see a window here in our church? (Wait for responses.) That's right. There are several windows near where we are sitting. What are windows for? (Wait for responses.) Very good! Windows let in light, and let us look out if we are inside, and let us look in if we are outside.

(Hold up a Bible.) What is this? (Wait for responses.) Right. The Bible is like a window. When we read and listen to stories from the Bible, we see how people lived and worked hundreds of years ago. For example, the Bible has a story about a woman who was very poor. She had little money, but she wanted to help her church, so she gave what she had to the church. What this story means is that no matter how much or how little we have, God will be happy if we share with others.

Lord, thank you for the Bible and the stories that teach us to share. Amen.

Notes

. . . .

. . . .

. . . .

. . . .

Saying Thank You
Psalm 100:4

Material: a stick of gum or a piece of hard candy for each child

Last week we discussed windows and what they are used for. Today we will talk about saying "thanks." (Give each child gum or candy.) Very good! Thank you for saying "thanks". When people give us something, we say "thank you," don't we? Saying "thanks" or "thank you" lets people know we appreciate what they have done for us.

When we say the blessing at mealtime, we are saying "thank you" to God for the food provided for us to eat. When we say our prayers, we are saying "thank you" to God for the gift of life and for loving us.

Telling our parents we love them is another way of saying "thank you" for taking care of us and keeping us safe. God likes for us to say "thank you."

Next week we will talk about our church family.

Thank you, God, for your world and for our lives. Amen.

Notes

. . . .

. . . .

. . . .

. . . .

Our Church Family
Ephesians 3:15

Materials: church directory; a picture of a church and people entering it for each child

Today we will talk about out church family. (Hold up church directory.) What is this? (Wait for responses.) Yes, this is a picture book of the members of our church family. Some of you and your families are in this book.

What is a family? What is this? Good! A family can be people who live together and who love each other and who look after each other. For example, Mary is my wife, and Suzanne and David are my children. We are a family.

But family can also mean people who believe alike, who love one another but live in different houses—like our church family. There are many families living in many different houses, but when we all come to church, or God's House, we are family—family because we love and care for one another.

You are a member of your personal family with your mom, dad, brothers, and sisters. You are also a member of this church family. You are loved here.

Thank you, God, for our church family. Amen.

Notes

. . . .

. . . .

. . . .

. . . .

Growing Up

Hosea 14:5; 2 Peter 3:18

Materials: a flower for each child

Do you remember what we talked about last week? (Wait for responses.) Great! You have good memories. Today we will talk about this. (Hold up a flower). What is it? (Wait for responses.) Right—a flower.

What makes a flower grow? (Wait for responses.) Good. So a flower has to have dirt, rain, and sunlight to grow and become beautiful and useful. What are flowers good for? (Wait for responses.) We can admire their beauty. Some flowers provide food for insects such as bees. Flowers also provide seeds that can take root and grow more flowers.

Just as flowers grow, so do we. What makes us grow? (Wait for responses.) Yes. We need food and water and light and shelter and love and care. Just like this flower, each one of us can grow to be beautiful and useful in God's world.

God, thank you for our wonderful world. Amen.

Notes

. . . .

. . . .

. . . .

. . . .

God's Recipe
Galatians 5:22; John 13:34

Materials: a cookbook; a cookie recipe for each child

Who remembers what the children's sermon was about last week? (Wait for responses.) Very good. How smart you are!

(Hold up the cookbook) Who knows what this is? That's right. A book of recipes. So—what is a recipe? (Wait for responses.) It is instructions or directions or rules on how to make something—like cookies or cakes or pies or hamburgers.

How many of you have helped your mom make cookies? (Wait for responses.) I'll bet you followed a recipe and the recipe listed the ingredients or things you put in to make the cookies—things like sugar, butter, flour, salt, eggs, nuts, and chocolate chips. Then you mixed all that together, put the cookies in the oven, cooked them awhile, took them out, let them cool, and then you ate them. Right?

God has a recipe He wants all of us to follow. It goes like this: Take all boys and girls of all colors—black, white, brown, yellow, and red—and all moms and dads of all colors—black, white, brown, yellow, and red—and have them live and work together in peace and love. God wants all His children to respect each other and to help each other.

Next week we will talk about helping each other.

Oh God, help us to work together in peace and love. Amen.

Notes

. . . .

. . . .

. . . .

. . . .

Helping
Isaiah 41:6

Materials: a candy cane for each child; a walking cane

(Hold up a walking cane.) What is this? (Wait for responses.) Very good—a walking stick or cane. What is it used for? (Wait for responses.) Right. To help people walk. Learning to help people is very important.

How many of you help your mom and dad at home? (Wait for responses.) What kind of chores or jobs do you have at home? (Wait for responses.) Excellent! Let's see, some of us pick up our toys, some of us help set the table for meals, some of us clean our rooms, some of us help in the yard, some of us help wash the car, and some of us take out the garbage.

When we help our parents and our teachers and our friends, we are kind of like a walking cane. We make the work easier for others. God likes for us to be helpers. Remember the little boy who shared his fish and bread with Jesus. He was a big helper!

Help us, God, to be good helpers. Amen.

Notes

. . . .

. . . .

. . . .

. . . .

Trees in God's World
Deuteronomy 20:19

Materials: a picture of a tree for each child

Remember what we talked about last week? (Wait for responses.) Great! What a smart bunch you are.

(Hold up a picture of a tree.) What is this? (Wait for responses.) Very good. It is indeed a picture of a tree. When I was a little boy, I liked to climb the fig tree in my grandmother's backyard. Not only could I pick figs to eat when they were in season, but I could see my friend's house when I climbed to the top of the tree. That was lots of fun.

What do you see when you climb trees? (Wait for responses.) What grows on trees? (Wait for responses.) True! Figs, apples, pears, oranges, bananas, grapefruit, peaches and other fruits, and even things like pine cones and flowers.

God's world is filled with growing things, and many of God's creations grow on trees. This week remember to look on trees to see what is growing on them. And also remember that the tree and what is growing on it are part of God's world!

Thank you, God, for trees and all your creation. Amen.

Notes

. . . .

. . . .

. . . .

. . . .

What Are Band-Aids For?

Luke 10:34

Materials: Band-Aids with pictures on them for each child.

(Hold up a Band-Aid.) What is this? (Wait for responses.) What are Band-Aids used for? (Wait for responses.) That's right! Band-Aids are used to put on hurt places. Sometimes we fall and scrape our arms, and sometimes we scratch our knees, and sometimes we cut ourselves. After we clean the hurt place, we can put a Band-Aid on it.

Band-Aids are used on the outside of our bodies—like on a cut finger. Sometimes, though, we have hurt places on the inside. We may feel sad because one of our friends moved, or our pet died, or someone may have hurt our feelings.

What do we do when we hurt on the inside? (Wait for responses.) That's right. We talk to our moms and dads, and they help us understand and make us feel better. Sometimes they help us talk to God about it in our prayers. Sometimes we get a hug. Hugs make us feel better, don't they? I want to give each of you a hug this morning.

Thank you, God, for people who help us make our hurt places better. Amen.

Notes

. . . .

. . . .

. . . .

. . . .

Going around in Circles
Proverbs 18:24

Today we will talk about riding on a merry-go-round or a carousel. Raise your hand if you have ridden on a carousel. Good. It was fun—right? Well, what if you rode that merry-go-round over and over and over again? After awhile it might get boring because you always arrived right back where you started.

Now life is a little bit like riding that carousel. We get up in the morning, eat breakfast, go to preschool, kindergarten, or school, do our work, eat lunch, take a rest, do our work, go home, eat a snack, play a little, do our chores, prepare our homework, eat supper, take a bath, and go to bed. We follow that routine five days a week. It is kind of like going in a circle.

In order to keep from being bored and always arriving back at the same place we started, we have to stay alert and look for new things to do, new games to play, and new friends to make. Even though we may seem to be going in a circle, we can make that circle larger and larger by doing new things and meeting new people and making new friends.

Look around you now. Is there anyone in this group you don't know? Maybe this is the time to make a new friend.

God, help us to learn something new every day. Amen.

Notes

. . . .

. . . .

. . . .

. . . .

Church Words

Church
Ephesians 5:25

Materials: a small plastic or paper church *or* a picture of a church for each child

Today we will talk about a word we hear several times a week—church. We are in church now, aren't we? Church is a place, a building(s), and we come to this building every Sunday to worship God.

Church, however, is more than just this building. It is the people that come to this building that give meaning to this place. It is like your school. School is a place or building where you and your friends play, make things, learn to read and write, and enjoy being with each other. You help make school what it is—a place to learn. Now, if the school were empty all of the time, what good would it be?

The same is true of church. If our church (or any church) were empty on Sunday (and other times), what good would it do in our community?

Next week we will talk about another church word—attendance—coming to church.

Thank you, God, for our church. Amen.

Notes

. . . .

. . . .

. . . .

. . . .

Attendance
Psalm 122:1

Last week we talked about what the word church means. Today we will talk about another church word—attendance. Church attendance means coming to church. At my house on Sunday morning everyone is moving around pretty fast. Everyone wants to use the bathroom at one time, everyone wants to get dressed at the same time, and everyone wants to pile into the car at the same time. I'll bet things at your house are the same.

It takes a lot of energy to get ready to come to church. Sometimes it is easier to stay at home. But if we don't come to Sunday School and church, what will we miss? (Wait for responses; offer help if needed.) That's right. We would not get to see our friends, and we would miss seeing our Sunday School teacher, and we would not get to have our children's time together. You and I would not get to see each other. I would miss you! This time together every Sunday morning in big church is very important to me. When I don't get to see you and talk with you, I become very sad and really miss you. God misses you when you are not here, too.

Next week we will talk about another church word—sanctuary—the place where we are right now.

Thank you, God, for the opportunity of coming to church. Amen.

Notes

. . . .

. . . .

. . . .

. . . .

Sanctuary
Exodus 25:8

Last week we discussed the church word attendance—coming to church. The church word we will talk about today is sanctuary. That's a big word, isn't it? When your parents say they will meet in the sanctuary, they mean the place where we are right now. The sanctuary is where the choir sings on Sunday and where the minister preaches the sermon.

It's easy to confuse the word church with sanctuary. All of the rooms and buildings we use are referred to as "the church." For example, where you have your Sunday School lesson is part of our church building.

One of the ways you can tell this is the sanctuary is to look at what is in it. The pews are where we sit. The pulpit is what the minister puts his/her Bible on when s/he preaches the sermon. The collection plates remind us that we should give some of our money to God. The choir sits there (point to it) and helps us with the music that tells us about God and the world. The flowers remind us of God's world and the beauty of nature. The cross helps us remember the story of Jesus. And the piano and organ remind us of the beautiful music that comes from them.

Next week we will talk about another church word—Bible.

Lord, thank you for this beautiful place to learn about you. Amen.

Notes

. . . .

. . . .

. . . .

. . . .

Bible

Matthew 24:35; Hebrews 4:12

Materials: a Bible for each child

Last week we talked about the church word sanctuary or the meeting place in the church building used for worship—what we are doing right now. Today we will talk about another church word—Bible.

The Bible is more than just a word, isn't it? The Bible is a book. In fact, the Bible is 66 different books all bound together. (Show children your Bible.) Each book in the Bible is a chapter book. When you learn to read, you will want to read books that have separate chapters. In fact, I bet some of you are already reading books with chapters.

The Bible is the main book people read when they want to know about God and Jesus. When you go to school, the teacher tells you the books you should read so that you can learn what you need to know. You have books about reading, math, spelling, science, history, and social studies. Studying the information in those books will make you smarter. In the same way, as followers of God and Jesus, we need to study the stories in the Bible so we will know more.

Next week we will talk about another word used by church people—member, church members.

Thank you, God, for the Bible. Amen.

Notes

· ·

· ·

· ·

· ·

Member
Romans 12:5

Last week we talked about the Bible, one of the words we use in church. Today we will talk about another church word—church member. The word member means being a part of a group or belonging to a group. Each one of you belongs to one or more groups. You are a member, for example, of your school class, your Scout troop, your Sunday School class, and your choir. Some of you are members of a sports team such as soccer, baseball, basketball, hockey, or football.

Being a member means being part of a group. Each of you is a part of our own church family here at _____. You belong here, and you are a part of all we do and think about. Just as you are a part of the Smith family or the Horn family or the Jones family, you are a part of this church family. (At this point you may want to say a word about general membership requirements of your specific denomination/congregation—but remember the age group before you.)

Next week we will talk about another church word—minister.

Lord, thank you for groups like our church that we can belong to. Amen.

Notes

. . . .

. . . .

. . . .

. . . .

Minister
1 Corinthians 12:28

Last week's church word was member—church member. Today's church word is minister (or priest). Who is our minister? (Wait for responses.) What does she do? (Wait for responses.) That's right. She preaches sermons and visits people who are sick. She also does a lot that we don't know about. Ministers are people who believe God wants them to preach, teach, and show people what God is like.

Ministers study about God a long time, and they keep on studying about God even when they go to work in a church. They have to study hard, just like you do in school, so they will know what to teach us on Sunday.

Some churches have two or three or four or more ministers. (Name the ministers in your church, and tell what each does.) Some churches have ministers who mostly preach and teach. Some churches also have ministers who just work with the choirs and music programs. And some churches have ministers who work mostly with the children or teenagers. Let's all say a big "thank you" to our ministers!

Next week our church word is believe.

Thank you, God, for our ministers. Amen.

Notes

. . . .

. . . .

. . . .

. . . .

Believe
John 20:29

Materials: a rubber or plastic ball

What was last week's church word? (Wait for responses.) Excellent! It was minister. This week's church word is believe.

There is a story in the Bible about a man named Thomas. Jesus told Thomas there are two ways to believe. One is to see things for yourself. For example, this is a ball (show ball to children). How do you know this is a ball? (Wait for responses.) Right. You know this is a ball; you believe this is a ball because you can see it.

Here, pass the ball around. Now, look at the ball. Touch it. Smell it. Feel its roundness. When you get on a hard surface, you can bounce it. It's a ball because it looks, feels, smells, and bounces like a ball. So, it is easy to believe this a ball because we can see it and hold it.

Jesus also said that there is another way to believe, and that is to know something or someone is real but not to see or touch it/them. This is hard, isn't it? But we do this kind of believing all of the time. For example, when our parents and teachers show us pictures of mountains, rivers, and people in other countries, we know they are real, even though we have not seen them. We know they are real because we believe our parents and teachers tell us the truth. We know those rivers, mountains, and people are real because we have seen rivers, mountains, and people on trips we have taken.

Have your parents ever picked you up? They don't drop you, do they? They hold you tight. You believe they will not let you go. That's the way God is. God holds us real tight and, like mom and dad, won't let us go.

Next week our church word is faith.

Thank you, God, for being able to believe in you. Amen.

Notes

. . . .

. . . .

Faith

2 Corinthians 5:7

Last week we discussed the church word believe. Today our church word is faith. Faith and believe are words that mean almost the same thing. Remember last week we said that we could believe in at least two ways. One, we can believe in something or someone like the ball I passed around last week because we can see it, feel it, and play with it. Two, we can believe in things (rivers, mountains, boats, cars, etc.) and people we hear about but do not see or talk to because our parents and teachers tell us those things and people exist and are real.

In other words, we have faith in what our parents and teachers tell us, even though we don't have any proof that they are telling us the truth. The Bible tells the story of Noah. God told Noah to build a big boat because it was going to rain a great deal, and he and his family and the animals would need to be safe from the flood. Noah built the boat, even though he had no proof that all that water was going to come. Noah had faith that the rain was coming, so he constructed the boat.

So faith is about trust and loyalty. We accept or have faith in what our parents and what our teachers say because we trust them and are loyal to them. For example, when our parents tell us that accepting rides with strangers is dangerous, we believe them because we have faith in their advice. We know they will tell us what is best for us. We know they will keep us safe and secure.

Next week our church word is hope.

Thank you, God, for parents who teach us about faith. Amen.

Notes

. . . .

. . . .

. . . .

Hope
Galatians 5:5; 2 Thessalonians 2:16

Last week our church word was faith. Today our church word is hope. Hope is sometimes hard to understand. Hope means looking forward to something and believing we will receive it. For example, you may ask for a bicycle for Christmas, and when your friends ask you if you will get a bicycle from Santa, you probably say, "I hope so!" What you mean is that you don't have the bicycle now, but you expect Santa to bring it to you.

In church we use the word hope a great deal. We say, for example, that we hope going to church will help make us better individuals. In other words, we hope that going to church will remind us of what God wants us to do and how God wants us to live.

When we say that our hope is in God, we're saying that we believe obeying God's rules of loving Him and loving each other is the way we should live each day of our lives.

Next week our church word will be love.

Thank you, God, for hope. Amen.

Notes

. . . .

. . . .

. . . .

. . . .

Love
John 3:16; 15:17

Our church word last week was hope. Today we will talk about a church word we hear a lot about—love. We use the word love to describe many things. We say "I love you," or "I love my cat," or "I love ice cream," or "I love to go to the circus," or "I love to play soccer," or "I love to watch TV," or "I love my church," or "I love God." Each of these "I love yous" means that we like that thing or person a great deal. For another example, when we say we love our moms and dads, we are saying they mean so much to us that we would do anything we could to help them. When your mom and dad say they love you, they are saying you are special and that they will take care of you and keep you safe and secure.

The Bible tells us that God loves us very much and that He sent His son, Jesus, to teach us how to live. Jesus said we should love each other and look after each other.

Next week our church word is grace.

Thank you, God, for loving every one of us. Amen.

Notes

. . . .

. . . .

. . . .

. . . .

Grace

2 Timothy 1:9

Materials: a small piece of candy or an appropriate gift for each child

Last week our church word was love. This week our church word is grace. Now that's an interesting word, isn't it?

Grace can be a person's name, can't it? But it is also a word that is used in church. When we hear one of our ministers or church teachers say something like "by God's grace we are all His children," we may not know what that means. The best way to remember what the word grace means is to think about a gift.

For example, pretend you have been playing with a friend and you return home and find a big chocolate bar on the kitchen table with your name on it. Your mom says, "It's for you." You are so happy. You give her a big hug and say "thanks." That chocolate bar is a gift from your mom. You did not ask for it. You did not work to earn it. She just gave it to you. You did not have to pay money for it. Your mom just freely gave you that big, wonderful, tasty piece of candy!

So when someone says "by God's grace we are His children," remember that the word grace means "gift." So we are God's children because God freely claims us as His children and loves us without reservation. We do not have to pay money to be loved by God, and we do not have to ask God to love us. God's love is God's gift to us.

Next week our church word is forgiveness.

Thank you, God, for your gift of love. Amen.

Notes

. . . .

. . . .

. . . .

Forgiveness
Daniel 9:9

Last week our church word was grace. Today it is forgiveness. Pretend your dad told you to pick up your toys and to clean up your room. Just as you started to pick up your toys, your best friend knocked on the door and said he wanted to play. So the two of you played for the rest of the afternoon. At supper dad asked if you had done what he asked you to do. More than likely you would say something like, "Oh dad, I forgot. Please forgive me. I promise to pick up my toys and clean my room right now!" And dad might say, "Okay. I forgive you. After supper will be alright."

You may have felt much better after dad said he forgave you and you could do your chore after supper. Forgiveness means we are not punished for doing wrong and that we won't be reminded again and again of what we did. The Bible talks a lot about forgiveness and tells us we should forgive one another because God has forgiven us.

A good way to remember what forgiveness means is to think about a chalkboard with lots of writing on it. The teacher takes an eraser and erases all the writing from the chalkboard, and it is clean. When we are forgiven, the bad things we did are erased or wiped clean. And when we forgive someone who has hurt us or taken something that belonged to us, we try to erase those things from our minds and start anew with them.

Next week our church word is missionary.

God, thank you for forgiving us. Amen.

Notes

. . . .

. . . .

. . . .

. . . .

Missionary
Acts 13:1ff

Last week our church word was forgiveness. This morning we will talk about a church word you have all heard many times—missionary. What is a missionary? (Wait for responses.) Very good! A missionary is someone on a mission (trip) with a message. That is, a missionary is a minister or a person who tells people about God's love.

We often think about missionaries as people who go far away to other places, like China, to live with and teach those individuals about Jesus. But missionaries can also live right here in our town (city).

Let's pretend you want to tell your grandparents about what you did and learned in Vacation Bible School. You want to show them the work (bird house, doll house, Bible verse tree, etc.) you did. But your grandmother and granddaddy live a long way from your house. So you and your family decide to make the trip to your grandparents so you can tell them the good news about what you learned about God and God's world in Vacation Bible School.

In taking that trip to your grandparents to tell them about what you learned in Vacation Bible School, you are doing what missionaries do—taking the word about God and God's world to people who need and want to know.

The Bible tells about missionaries like Paul who traveled all around telling people about what he had learned about Jesus and about God.

Thank you, God, for missionaries who tell people about you. Amen.

Notes

. . . .

. . . .

. . . .

. . . .

Special Days

New Beginnings
Galatians 6:15; Revelation 21:5

Materials: notebook with 365 pages for each child

Last Sunday was the last Sunday in the year____. Today is the first Sunday in the new year, _____. Celebrating the beginning of a new year is very exciting. There will be 365 days in this year and 52 Sundays. Each day in the new year is like a page in a book. I'll bet each of you has a lot of books you like to look at or read. Some of your books have a few pages and some of your books have many pages.

Think of this new year as a book with 365 pages and 52 of those pages will be Sunday pages. Every day of this new year you will do things that you did the day before, like eat, brush your teeth, play, go to school, and sleep. But every day you will do something different. So each day of this new year will be a different experience for you. Each day will be like a brand new page in your notebook, and on the first day of each new week you can come to Sunday School and church.

How about this for an idea? I want to give each one of you a notebook with 365 pages in it. Every day I want you to put something that's important to you on each page. You may want to draw a picture, write a sentence or two, or paste something on the page. At the end of the year you can look back over each page, and see what was important to you on that day. And also at the end of the year you can put that notebook away, and on New Year's Day you can start all over again.

God tells us that new beginnings are good!

Thank you God for new beginnings. Amen.

Notes

. . . .

. . . .

Living Like Jesus
Luke 24:5-6

Materials: two flowers—one dead and one fresh

Today is Easter Sunday. We know it is a special day because of the beautiful flowers and pretty Easter dresses the girls are wearing and the spiffy outfits the guys have on. But Easter means more than nice clothes, candy, bunnies, and egg hunts. Easter means that Jesus is alive and that we should have no fear of death.

You remember the story of Jesus. He was a preacher who walked around his country telling people that God loved them and that they should love God and one another. He also told the people he met that they should spend their time doing good deeds like helping the poor, feeding the hungry, and visiting the sick.

Jesus made a lot of important people mad when he told them to worship God and not to worship kings and rulers. These people killed Jesus, but he did not stay dead. He came out of his grave and returned to his friends.

(Hold the dead flower in one hand and the fresh flower in the other.) What do I have in my hands? (Wait for responses.) That's right! I have a dead flower and a live flower. It's not much fun to look at the dead flower, is it? Looking at this beautiful Easter lily that is alive and fresh is a real treat.

Easter is about life, about being alive and trying to live by the rules Jesus taught us. Jesus wants us to be glad we are alive, and he wants us to live by his rules.

Thank you, God, for Jesus who taught us how to live. Amen.

Notes

. . . .

. . . .

. . . .

What Do Mothers Do?

Psalm 113:9; Ephesians 6:1-2

Today is Mother's Day. This is the one Sunday out of 52 Sundays in the year that we especially honor and remember our moms. Mothers are wonderful, aren't they? They can do so many things. Let's take a minute and see if we can name some of the things moms do. (Wait for responses.) You are right! Moms have babies, and they care for us when we are sick, and they cook and clean the house, and they work and make money to buy us clothes and food. And they read to us, and they teach us about manners and about right and wrong.

We have named some of the things moms do. Now let's talk about some of the things we can do for our moms—not just today, but every day. (Wait for responses.) Good! We can obey our moms—do what they tell us to do. We can keep our toys and books picked up, and make our beds and clean our rooms, and help with our little brothers and sisters. We can take out the garbage, help with the pets, and set the table for meals. And we can give our mom a big hug and tell her we love her.

It pleases God when we honor and help our moms.

God, thank you so much for our mothers. Amen.

Notes

. . . .

. . . .

. . . .

. . . .

What Do Fathers Do?
Ephesians 6:1-2

What is today? (Wait for responses.) Yes! It's Father's Day, the one Sunday in the 52 Sundays in the year when we pay special attention to our dads. What would we do without dads? They help us in so many ways. Let's think together about what our dads do. (Wait for responses.) Very good! Dads work to make money for our family. They help with the housework, and mow the grass, and stay up at night with us when we are sick. They take us to the movies and to ballgames, watch TV with us, read to us, and teach us about right and wrong.

Let's see if we can name some of the ways we can make today and every day special for our dads. (Wait for responses.) Excellent! We can obey our dads when they tell us what we should do. And we can help dad with the housework and the yard work. We can help with washing and cleaning the car, and take dad a snack when he is doing book work at night, and let him take a nap on Sunday afternoon. Most of all, we can give dad a hug and tell him we love him.

It pleases God when we honor and help our dads.

Thank you, God, for our dads. Amen.

Notes

. . . .

. . . .

. . . .

. . . .

All Work Can Be God's Work

Colossians 3:17

This weekend we are celebrating labor or work. That's what labor is—working. Maybe you went to a Labor Day party this weekend where friends got together to have a good time. When we think about labor or work, we usually remember people who have jobs that help us: people like postmen, firefighters, police officers, nurses, doctors, teachers, ministers, druggists, waiters and waitresses, carpenters, and the people who check us out of the line at the grocery store.

In God's world there are many different kinds of jobs, and all of them are important. The doctor's job is to help us get well, and that is certainly important. But if our car won't start, we soon find out how important mechanics are. Teachers are important because they help us learn what we don't know. But without farmers, we would not have enough food to eat. And lawyers are important because they help us with many of our problems. But just think how sad we would be if all of the people who make candy to sell to us quit making candy!

Everyone who works in God's world is special and needed. The jobs you do at home to help mom and dad are very important. And it pleases God when you work hard and do your job well.

Thank you, God, for work and those who work. Amen.

Notes

· ·

· ·

· ·

· ·

Being Thankful

Psalm 100:4-5

This Sunday we will think about being thankful—because it is Thanksgiving week. What does Thanksgiving Day mean to you? (Wait for responses.) That's good! Thanksgiving does mean having turkey for lunch. And it means we remember the Pilgrims and the first Thanksgiving Day. Thanksgiving means that some of us get a holiday. But Thanksgiving is more than a turkey dinner, more than a holiday, and more than remembering the Pilgrims.

Thanksgiving is a time to thank God for all the good things in our lives. We should be thankful for our families, and our country, and for the freedom to worship God in our church. We should thank God for our church and our Sunday School teachers and the people who come to our church and make up our church family. We can also be thankful that we can study about Jesus each Sunday.

Thanksgiving is a good time to say a special "thank you" to our moms and dads for all they do for us.

We are thankful, God, for all your blessings. Amen.

Notes

. . . .

. . . .

. . . .

. . . .

A Special Baby
Luke 2:10ff

Materials: a doll wrapped in a blanket

Today is one of the most special Sundays in the whole year. Today we talk about Christmas—the birthday of Jesus. (Hold up the doll). What is this? That's right. It is a baby doll. Babies are cute, aren't they? I'll bet some of you have a baby at your house. You know, not too long ago you looked just like this!

A long, long time ago a very special baby was born. His mother was named Mary, and his father was named Joseph. He was born in a cave (barn) because all of the hotels were full. His mom and dad were very proud of him, and they wanted to keep him safe and provide the things he needed to grow.

Joseph, Jesus' dad, was a carpenter. He made things out of wood. Jesus had some brothers, and they played in their yard and sometimes even in their dad's carpenter shop. Jesus knew that he wanted to be a preacher from the time he was a little boy. He probably practiced preaching on his family.

Jesus became the most famous preacher in the world. We come to church to study about him. Even though Jesus was born in a barn, he grew up to be a man whom we want to be like. He was kind, gentle, smart, caring, and giving. Christmas is Jesus' birthday. For our present to him today, let's promise each other that we will try to be more like Jesus—kind, caring, and giving.

Thank you, Oh God, for Jesus and for what he taught us. Amen.

Notes

. . . .

. . . .

. . . .

. . . .

Resources

Basics of Human Development

One of my favorite graduate school professors would say at the beginning of his classes, "Remember, all children are alike, and all children are different." The first few times I heard that mantra, I thought it to be simplistic and, of course, highly redundant. It was later in my study of human development that the profoundness of that statement engulfed me. Indeed, children are alike—they have similar physical, mental, and social characteristics—but those characteristics develop according to each child's individual timetable, influenced by both heredity and environment.

For example, Max and Marie are 4 years old. They are from similar socioeconomic backgrounds, attend the same preschool, and go to the same church. Marie is tall; Max is short. Marie is slender; Max is chubby. Marie knows her colors, can count to 10, can recite her phone number and her address, and is agile and very social. Max, on the other hand, does not know his colors, gets mixed up in counting to 10 and in reciting his phone number and address, and is clumsy and a little shy around people other than his family members.

What's wrong with Max? The answer could be: nothing. Marie is progressing according to her schedule, and Max according to his. A developmentalist assessing Max would consider the data from his growth chart, family history, socioeconomic background, and anecdotal records from caretakers and teachers. The fact that Max is a male (males are, until the teen years, often slower in reaching some developmental milestones than females) would also be taken into consideration. Assuming there are no major physical, cognitive, or social problems evident, Max's caregivers would probably be urged to continue to provide an enriched environment for him, not to push him too hard, and to bring him back for a checkup in 6-12 months. Although Max seems to "lag" behind his peers in development, most likely he will "catch up" by the teen years.

On the other hand, if variables such as lower socioeconomic standing, family history of genetic disorders, prolonged illness, and nutritional deficiency are involved, both Marie and Max's developmental profile could be very different. Immediate medical, educational, and social intervention would be warranted. Every child is similar, but every child is also very different!

Information Gathering

People who study children's development and provide information for public consumption glean their information primarily from case studies, naturalistic observations, and tests and surveys. The scientific method provides additional information about how children function in society.

A case study involves collecting a great deal of information from tests, observations, and personal interviews with one person or sometimes a small group. Both therapists and researchers use this method often. Much information about children can be gleaned by observing them in their natural habitats, especially the playground, school, and sometimes the home setting. Tests and surveys permit developmentalists to generate a critical amount of comparative data such as height, weight, socioeconomic standing, and motor and play behaviors. The scientific method involves controlled testing, often within a laboratory setting, the statement of a hypothesis, sampling procedures, independent and dependent variables, and the reporting of information in statistical form.

Terminology

The study of children involves not only research procedures, but also the use of certain words and phrases in specific ways. The following glossary explains some terms commonly used in human development theory.

- *Ages* are guidelines used to describe physical, cognitive, and social growth. Chronological age descriptors are not fixed; they are flexible and depend upon each child's individual response to his/her genes and environment.

- *Cognitive growth* refers to the normal changes in neuronal configurations that permit individuals to engage in increasingly more complex behavior. It is the same as mental growth, and is often assessed by both observation and psychological tests.

- *Development* applies to changes over time.

- *Developmental lag* is the difference between expected and actual behavior at a certain age.

• *Developmental processes* include physical, cognitive, and social functions.

• *Developmentalists* are professionals who usually work in the academic fields of education, psychology, medicine, and/or social work and are especially trained or educated in the behavior of infants, children, and adolescents.

• *Developmentally appropriate* refers to educational practices that seek to match age appropriateness (the approximate age at which children are ready to perform certain physical, cognitive, and social tasks) with individual appropriateness (relating age appropriateness to an individual child's unique personality, learning style, and family background).

• *Egocentric* means believing everyone thinks as you do.

• *Early childhood* is the period of 3-6 years.

• *Infancy* lasts from birth to age 2.

• *Interactive* relates to genes and environment acting upon one another in developmental processes.

• *Late childhood* covers ages 9-10.

• *Middle childhood* is the time span from 7-8 years.

• *Nature* concerns the argument that physical, cognitive, and social behaviors are primarily dependent upon genetic endowment.

• *Nurture* relates to the argument that one's physical, cognitive, and social behaviors are primarily shaped by the environment.

• *Periods* are the various developmental age spans.

• *Physical growth* embraces the actual measurable changes occurring in the body such as head circumference, weight, and height.

• *Social growth* is a broad term referring to the changes that occur in interpersonal relationships, the acquiring of a sense of morality, emotional responses to internal and external stimuli, the exploration of gender roles, the formulation of an identity, and overall personality development.

- *Stages* are distinct sequential periods of growth and development, with physical, cognitive, and social behavior being qualitatively different in each stage. The stages are more discontinuous than continuous. In other words, each stage signals a different kind of person or behavior as opposed to a smooth, gradual, cumulative change. All individuals do not necessarily complete all stages.

- *Theories* are ideas that seek to explain human development phenomena and to make predictions about human behavior.

Trying to discern and understand childhood behavior is somewhat akin to working 10 crossword puzzles at one time, reading Einstein's theory of relativity, and waiting for the pot to boil. It can be done, but in the case of children's behavior, it takes patience, expertise, professional assistance and, most of all, a comprehension of the complexities that underlie human behavior. (See interpretive chart on p. 87)

Contexts for Development

Families

Most children begin life in a family context and there live out their biological and social stories. Family means something different in each culture and each subculture. Indeed, the form of the family in this country has changed dramatically in the last 40 years. The predominance of the nuclear family (father, mother, children) of the pre-1960s has been supplanted with other forms of the family. The blended family (his children, her children, their children) is a common form of the family today. The single-parent family is the most rapidly emerging form of the family. At least 50% of the children born in the 1980s will live in a single-parent home, and perhaps as many as 75% of the next generation will live in a single-parent family.

It is reasonable to ask why the form of the American family has changed so rapidly in the last 40 years. One primary reason relates to the expectations of the culture. Society no longer requires the nuclear family; divorce is accepted; and both parents working is common. The culture's expectations of the family changed in part due to economic and political changes. As

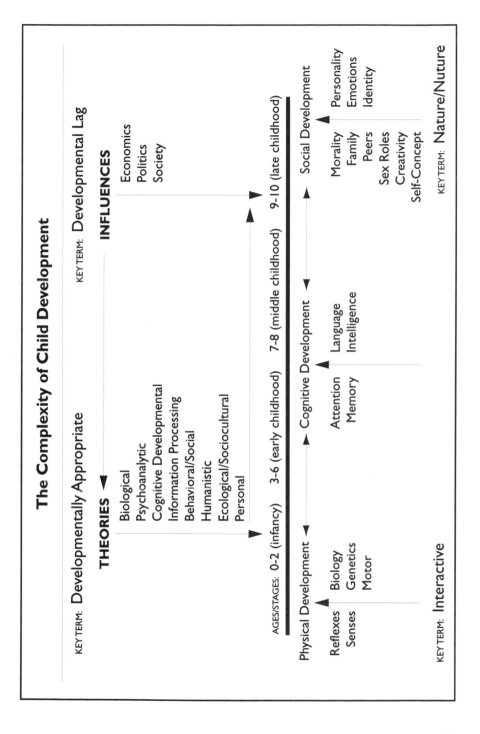

The Complexity of Child Development

KEY TERM: Developmentally Appropriate

KEY TERM: Developmental Lag

THEORIES

Biological
Psychoanalytic
Cognitive Developmental
Information Processing
Behavioral/Social
Humanistic
Ecological/Sociocultural
Personal

INFLUENCES

Economics
Politics
Society

AGES/STAGES: 0-2 (infancy)   3-6 (early childhood)   7-8 (middle childhood)   9-10 (late childhood)

Physical Development → Cognitive Development → Social Development

Biology
Genetics
Motor

Reflexes
Senses

Attention
Memory

Language
Intelligence

Morality
Family
Peers
Sex Roles
Creativity
Self-Concept

Personality
Emotions
Identity

KEY TERM: Interactive

KEY TERM: Nature/Nurture

individuals became more affluent, more mobile, and more detached from domestic tasks, they demanded more flexibility in the interpretation of values of family life. Specifically, as women entered the marketplace and gained independence, they could afford to divorce their spouses and establish homes on their own or merge their family with another. The more money parents made, the easier it was to afford child care. Thus, economics began to have a major say in defining child care. Specifically, individuals who were working and having children demanded that the marketplace and the political structure respond to their needs for assistance in child care. The women's movement also contributed to culture's consciousness concerning the rights of both genders. The "war on poverty" demanded that "welfare parents" go to work; but in order to meet that mandate, child care was essential.

Thus, all forms of the family (nuclear, blended, single parent) pressed politicians to recognize family diversity and to signal understanding by awarding monetary assistance to families with children. Currently, not only is the government responding in terms of the traditional aid programs to families, but also in mandating family leave policies and in urging businesses and industries to provide childcare programs. A look at the business and industrial landscape of the nation indicates that changes are in the making. For example, it is not unusual to find large businesses and industries providing child care for their employees, paid and unpaid family leave programs, and flexible work schedules for parents. There is little question that economics and politics play major roles in the formulation of the environment for families in America.

Another question concerning family change has to do with how easily transformations can occur. For instance, in some cultures, such as Asian, family traditions change slowly. Such traditions are passed on from generation to generation, and the culture as a whole supports enthusiastically those traditions. In American culture, however, change can occur rapidly. Reasons for this rapid change in the United States are many and varied:

• As a nation, it is less than 225 years old.
• Individualism and competitiveness have always been emphasized.
• Children and families have been economically based.
• There is little or no national consciousness about children.
• The economic output of adults is seen as the country's future, not the birth of children.
• Children are viewed as burdens, not as assets.
• Historically, children are not valued.

Schools

Rapid change in American culture, particularly regarding families, has raised the question of who is going to rear the children. Currently, at least 1 out of every 2 mothers with a child under age 5 works, and more than 2 of every 3 mothers with a child age 6-17 are employed outside the home. Assuming that the "both parents working" scenario will continue to be the norm, the question of who is going to rear the children becomes paramount.

Childcare literature suggests that the following locales provide some form of child care:

• public libraries and other public places such as hospitals and public parks
• streets/street families/gangs
• home alone—latchkey kids entertained and/or supervised by television, video games, siblings, and sometimes peers
• childcare centers
• public schools

Of all these childcare options, the public school system appears to be the one that will bear the major responsibility for childrearing in the United States in the years to come. The reasons are:

• Because public schools are owned by local governmental agencies, they do not appear as "big government" trying to rear children.

• Public schools (land and buildings) are available 24 hours a day, even though they are used only a maximum of 12-16 hours a day.

• Some public schools now enroll 4-year-olds, will soon have 3-year-old programs, and the prospect of 2-year-olds in the public schools of the future is feasible.

• Many public schools provide child care both before school and after school and on weekends. Breakfast and lunch programs represent an old childcare model. Innovative approaches include: early morning arrival programs, afterschool programs, weekend enrichment programs, and 12-month school calendars.

So who will rear the children? It appears that the culture, both from an economic and a political standpoint, will accept the public school as both teacher and parent more readily than they will programs mandated from Washington, D.C. It is much easier for parents to accept the parental role of schools because, after all, most of them went to public schools or a reasonable facsimile (private schools) and they, as taxpayers, own the schools.

The morality of the question of "who is going to rear the children?" can be debated ad infinitum. But the point here is that in the last 40 years, Americans have embraced drastic changes in childrearing practices. Society has moved from the nuclear family as the standard to the single-parent family as the norm. The culture has progressed from one parent working to both parents working. Whereas 40 years ago most mothers stayed home, now most mothers and fathers work. Therefore . . .

• Who will take care of the children?
• What is the church doing to assist parents with this perplexing question?
• What can children's sermons do to address these questions?

Theories of Human Development

Economics, politics, and the culture provide the general context in which children play out the dance between biology and environment. The dynamics of that dance are influenced greatly by theories, or ideas and assumptions that are organized in such a way as to give answers about why children grow and develop the way they do. There are numerous categories of theories used to explain human behavior. Eight categories of theories help explain why children behave as they do. These categories are: biological theories, psychoanalytic theories, learning theories, cognitive approaches, sociocultural theories, humanistic theories, faith development theories, and personal theories. These theories are highly complex and involve years of work by the theorists. An effort will be made here, however, to summarize the salient points of each theory in an attempt to provide the reader with a glimpse of the particular paradigm and to offer interpretive charts of the more complex theories.

Biological Theories

Arnold Gesell

Maturational theory, which is based in biology, stresses a view of human behavior that emphasizes the orderly unfolding of development. The physician Arnold Gesell (1880–1961) made this theory particularly popular in the first half of the 20th century. Many have seen the Gesell growth and development charts that emphasize and describe the ages at which different behaviors emerge. Gesell and his followers believe that physical and cognitive skills develop in accordance with each child's internal timetable and that learning and experience have nothing to do with the emergence of a particular behavior such as crawling, walking, or running. In fact, Gesell maintains that learning occurs only after individuals are organically ready to learn. Thus, Gesell provides the term "readiness," which means that children cannot perform certain tasks until they are neurologically ready to perform them. The Gesell Readiness Charts were often used, for instance, to determine how old children should be before they begin to participate in reading, math, and science.

Konrad Lorenz

Physician Konrad Lorenz (1903–1989) also emphasized biology in his study of human development. His theory is referred to as ethology, which stresses the evolutionary basis for human behavior. One of Lorenz's primary contributions is the idea of "critical periods," meaning fixed periods in development during which certain behaviors emerge. From this idea came the current concepts of bonding, attachment, and learning windows. Some say, for instance, that language is best learned during the first 5 years and number concept during the first 4 years.

Human Genome Project

One of the most exciting developments in science today is the mapping of the human genome. Hardly a week passes without some startling announcement reaching the public concerning a finding regarding the human genetic code. Scientists are locating chromosomes and, sometimes, genes within chromosomes that are to some degree responsible for disease, illness, and behavior. Behavior genetics and neurobiological, neurophysiological, and neuropsychological approaches to explaining human behavior are augmenting and rewriting many of the existing human development theories.

*****

In summary, biological theories stress genetic structure as the primary cause of physical, cognitive, and even social behavior. Few people today, however, are purists in their theoretical orientation but tend rather to stress one dimension over another. Biological theorists would of course emphasize genetics over environment or nature over nurture.

Psychoanalytic Theories

Sigmund Freud

Sigmund Freud's (1856–1939) psychosexual theory of human development centered on energy and instincts. Freud believed that the mind and body consist of bodily energy and psychic energy and that these energies are interchangeable. He believed that energy pulsates in the body and eventually centers in a certain spot (for example, an erogenous zone). The point at which the energy focuses creates a need, and that need is transferred to the brain. The brain forms a mental representation of that bodily state or need (instinct), and the mental representation becomes known as a wish. At this point Freud's 3-part personality structure comes into focus (see p. 94).

The ID is the source of all instincts and energy in the personality system. It is always unconscious and is a result of biology. The ID is innate. It is selfish, demanding, and operates according to the pleasure principle; the ID always wants immediate gratification. The Ego is the moderator of the three personality components. The Ego seeks to operate on a reality level and influences the demands of the ID in appropriate ways that will not be punished. The Superego is the moral component of Freud's personality system. It praises children when they act in accordance with society's rules and rebukes them through anxiety and guilt when they fail to obey. Again, the Ego is located between the ID and the Superego. The Superego and Ego have a grounding in reality, whereas the ID is totally unconscious. There is a constant struggle between the ID and the Superego to dominate, while the Ego seeks to moderate acceptable solutions.

When the mental representation in the mind becomes a wish, anxiety is produced due to the pressure to fulfill the wish. The ID insists that its wishes be fulfilled immediately. The Superego is oftentimes horrified at the demands of the ID, and the Ego is caught in the middle seeking to moderate. Whenever the tension between the ID and the Superego becomes more than th Ego can handle, rather than have the Ego collapse (which is sometimes the case), defense mechanisms operate unconsciously. These defense mechanisms, such as repression, projection, reaction formation, displacement, and sublimation, offer acceptable substitutes to the ID, thus saving the Ego from severe damage.

Freud identified 4 stages and a latency period in his psychosexual explanation of human development. His stages are oral, anal, phallic, and genital; and a latency period lasts from about ages 5-12. Each of Freud's stages is associated with a particular part of the body. For example, in the oral stage (birth-1 year) the mouth is the location of pain or pleasure. In the anal stage (ages 1-3) children are pitted against their parents, specifically as parents attempt to toilet train the children. During the phallic stage (ages 3-5) the Oedipal Complex develops. According to Freud, little boys fall in love with their mothers, and little girls fall in love with their fathers. They are able to solve this unhealthy relationship by identifying with the parent of the opposite sex. If this identification takes place, then children successfully solve the Oedipal complex and develop a Superego. This Oedipal conflict is much less sharply defined with females than with males in the Freudian scheme.

Sigmund Freud's Theory

Ego and **Superego**
are partially conscious.

ID is totally
unconscious.

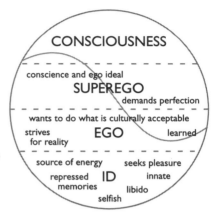

Structures of the Mind

(Selective) Ego Defenses are always
unconscious and are activated when the ego
is under attack from the ID or Superego.
Anxiety warns the Ego that it is in trouble,
and the defenses come to the rescue.

Repression: Unacceptable wishes/desires
from the ID are pushed from the conscious
mind to the unconscious mind. Example:
A sister's husband is desired, but such is not
acceptable to the Ego and is thus repressed.

Reaction Formation: Talking or
behaving in opposites. Example: "I would
not have a car like that if you gave it to
me." Meaning: "I want a car like that."

Projection: Attributing a desire, behavior,
or attitude to someone or something else.
Example: "Jane hates Tom." Meaning: "I
hate Tom."

Regression: Return to an earlier stage(s)/
behavior(s). Example: A teen begins to
behave like a 5-year-old.

Fixation: Growth ceases and the person
exhibits behaviors from a previous stage.
Example: A 9-year-old begins to put
everything in his mouth.

Stages

- Oral (birth-1 year)

- Anal (1-2 years)

- Phallic (3-5 years)

    Oedipus Complex
    Fear of Castration:
    Identification with the opposite sex
    parent solves the complex.

    Electra Complex
    Penis Envy:
    Identification with the opposite sex
    solves the complex.

    Outcome: Superego

- Latency (age 5-puberty)

- Genital (adolescence)

Freud's Methodology
    free association
    dreams
    analysis
    tranference

Basic Instincts

- Eros/Libido (life)

- Destruction (death)

Personality, according to Freud, is essentially established by the age of 5. From that point to ages 11 or 12 children are in a latency period during which no new activities emerge that will create problems. The genital stage begins at approximately age 12 or 13. At this juncture adolescents begin a socialization process that will take them into adult behavior.

In Freudian theory, if children progress through the stages normally and do not become fixated at a certain stage, they can expect to develop normal personalities. However, if instincts are overgratified or undergratified by parents, if defense mechanisms are not acquired, and if the Oedipal complex is solved unsatisfactorily, then individuals will experience tension-filled and anxiety-filled lives that will more than likely necessitate psychotherapy.

Freud's theory has had enormous impact on the culture. For example, simply extending the idea that what happens to children during the first 5 years emotionally will have a determining effect on them for the rest of their lives is a rather extraordinary claim. Childrearing practices and school curricula have in past years been based on Freudian concepts. For example, if children do not get to suck enough in infancy, they will suck other objects such as their thumbs, pens, pencils, etc. for the rest of their lives. If Johnny is not allowed to eat when he wants to, he will develop a neurotic personality and perhaps eat all of the time for comfort and satisfaction. And if Suzy is angry at school, she must be angry at her caregivers; therefore, she needs counseling and therapy.

Erik Erikson

Although he never earned a college or university degree, Erik Erikson (1902–1994) made numerous contributions to the interpretation of human behavior. He accepted many of Freud's ideas, but differed with Freud on several important aspects of human development. Erikson emphasized the social dimension of personality as opposed to the sexual dimension. He further postulated that development occurs over the lifetime rather than essentially ending at adolescence. Erikson's psychosocial theory has 8 stages during each of which people encounter a unique developmental task that confronts them with crises they must solve.

By crisis, Erikson means a turning point rather than a catastrophe. The more positively or adaptively persons solve crises, the healthier they will be. For example, if in the first year of life children are fed regularly and made to feel safe and secure, then they adopt an attitude of trust as opposed to an attitude of mistrust. The crisis of "trust versus mistrust" is solved according

Erikson's Psychosocial Stages vs. Freud's Psychosexual Stages

Psychosocial Stages (Crisis)		Ego Strengths or Virtue	Freud's Psychosexual Stages
Age	Adaptive/Maladaptive	If Solved Adaptively	
birth–1 year	TRUST vs. MISTRUST *Consistency in caregiving during the first year leads to trust. Inconsistency or negative care may cause mistrust.*	Hope	Oral
2-3 years	AUTONOMY vs. DOUBT *Children desire to try out their skills at their own pace and in their own way. However, overprotection or neglect may lead to doubt.*	Willpower	Anal
4-5 years	INITIATIVE vs. GUILT *Freedom in activities, attitudes, and language leads to initiative. Restrictions of such and parents' failure to be responsive to comments and questions lead to guilt.*	Purpose	Phallic
6-11 years	INDUSTRY vs. INFERIORITY *Making and doing things and being praised for trying and for accomplishing lead to industry. Limitation on such leads to inferiority.*	Competence	Latency

12-18 years	IDENTITY vs. ROLE CONFUSION *A recognition of stability within oneself leads to identity. Inability to establish such leads to role confusion.*	Fidelity	Genital
Young Adulthood	INTIMACY vs. ISOLATION *Focusing on another as opposed to self leads to intimacy. Isolation may occur when one becomes too combative.*	Love	
Middle Age	GENERATIVITY vs. STAGNATION *Looking out for the welfare of the next generation produces a sense of generativity. Self-centeredness leads to stagnation.*	Care	
Old Age	INTEGRITY vs. DESPAIR *Acceptance of life as it is leads to a sense of integrity. Believing that life could have been better leads to despair.*	Wisdom	

Erikson says psychosocial development proceeds according to "epigenetic principles" (emergence-ground plan) and that a primary objective of life is the search for identity. Erikson's work suggests that a well-developed, integrated ego will possess:

- Awareness
- Coherence
- Intentionality
- Mutuality

The concept of readaptation is useful when considering Erikson's theory. Readaption means that a person may, through exposure to a healthy person or social experience, revisit a stage in which maladaptive solutions have prevailed and solve the crisis or crises adaptively. For example, a 1st grade child may lack hope, willpower, and purpose, but 7 hours a school day with an aware, coherent, intentional, and caring teacher may cause that student to revisit prior stages and solve them adaptively. However, the reverse of this example can also occur.

Erikson's Methodology: direct observation, crosscultural comparison, and psychohistory

to the treatment they receive from their caregivers, thus emphasizing the social dimension. When children successfully resolve a crisis, they strengthen the Ego and are prepared to face the next crisis. If a crisis or "turning point" is unresolved or is "solved" maladaptively, then the ability to negotiate tasks at that stage or a later stage of life is affected.

According to Erikson, people make a profound difference. Parents, teachers, ministers, and peers can have a significant influence upon the way individuals solve crises at each stage of their lives. For example, if children who have been mistreated and abused in the first 5 or 6 years of life and are maladaptively coping with the challenges of life have a first grade teacher who engenders in them trust, autonomy, and initiative, through "readaptation" they can change from maladaptivity to adaptivity. Of course, the reverse is also true. Trustful, independent, challenging children can be paired with a caregiver, teacher, or minister who is abusive, hateful, shaming, and overly aggressive, and those children can change from adaptive to maladaptive behavior. Erikson's theory is a useful one, especially for persons in the helping and teaching professions.

Learning Theories

B. F. Skinner

B. F. Skinner (1904–1990) theorized that people behave the way they do based upon a concept he called "operant conditioning." Simply stated, the conscious or unconscious mind is not the key to behavior, but rather a person's environment. In order to change behavior, one needs to simply change the environment because all behavior is learned. For instance, if children cry and their caregivers pick them up, then according to Skinnerians, the children have been reinforced or rewarded and will more than likely repeat that behavior again.

When our grandson David Suthern and his parents moved to a small farm, he was fascinated with the deer, turkeys, and other wildlife he could see from the road leading to his house. One night, just after moving, David S. said to his dad, "Let's take a night ride and see the deer." His mom and dad thought the request was cute (and it was!), so they hugged him and took him for a "night ride." Night-riding, rain or shine, is now a part of the evening ritual at David Suthern's house! Skinnerians would say the origin of the night-ride behavior is easy to analyze. David Suthern made the request; it was positively reinforced and quickly became a routine behavior.

Operant conditioning, then, is the human organism acting upon the environment, and the environment's response to action determines whether or not the behavior will be repeated. Again, an example relating to this concept could involve children who do not want to go to church. Every time the family goes to church, the children cry, "pitch a fit," get sick, or become rigid and refuse to move. If their caregivers stay home with the children, the children have been reinforced in their behavior—which is what they wanted—and there is a great probability the behavior will occur again the next time the subject of church arises. As a matter of fact, through a process called "generalization," that behavior may spread to other similar situations in which the children do not wish to cooperate.

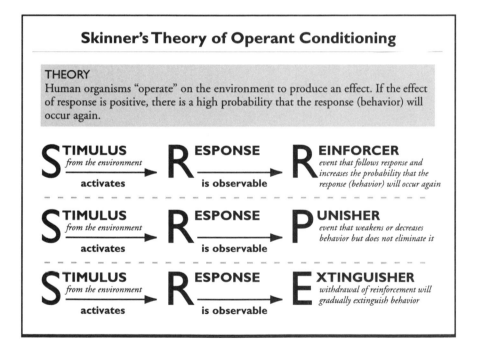

In order to change behavior, Skinnerians advocate rearranging experiences to emit behaviors that can and will be reinforced or rewarded. Behavior modification programs have emerged as effective ways to change behavior for some children, especially younger children. Following are some examples of behavior modification programs used in homes, schools, and churches:

• *Assertive discipline* involves the establishment of rules by the teacher or parent, consequences when rules are broken, and reinforcers for desired behavior.

• *Token economies* are symbolic reinforcement systems usually involving tokens that can be earned and applied to items valued by the children such as candy and chewing gum.

• *Behavioral contracts* are formalized documents between, for example, a parent and a child, that state in writing what the child will do and what the parent will do when those tasks are done.

• *Time out* is a method that removes a child from a reinforcing situation for a certain length of time.

Albert Bandura

For decades Albert Bandura (b. 1925) has researched the concept of observational learning. Bandura postulates that learning occurs vicariously. In other words, individuals are able to learn without having to experience the situation directly; they learn by observing the actions of others. Consider 3-year-old Sabrina who starts a car, all alone, and drives it into the corner of the garage. Who taught her to drive the car? Since she had never driven the car before, she did not have an opportunity to be reinforced for that behavior, so the obvious answer is that she had seen someone else drive the car, had stored the information in her memory, and on an occasion when a caregiver was not present in the car, "drove" it. Bandura's cognitive social learning theory of why people behave the way they do is highly instructive. In effect, Bandura's research has shown that people do what they observe others doing, not specifically what people tell them to do or have them to experience. Therefore, "do as I say not as I do" is highly ineffective!

Modeling is an essential construct in Bandura's thesis. His research has shown that children will imitate the behavior of models, particularly high status (entertainment personalities, parents, teachers) models without ever having experienced that behavior themselves. Consider, for instance, the 4-year-old child who will, after having watched a violent television program, punch his grandmother in the stomach and proclaim that he has just "decked" her.

Bandura's answer to why people behave as they do is not restricted to the environment or to the persons themselves or their behavior, but includes all three! Bandurans call this process "reciprocal determinism," which means that people act as they do because of multiple factors.

Cognitive Theories

Jean Piaget

Jean Piaget (1896–1980) was a child prodigy who received his Ph.D in biology when he was 21 years old. He was born, reared, and spent his entire professional career in Switzerland. Piaget believed that all individuals are born with the tendency to organize and to adapt. He postulated that from the earliest age, with exposure to the environment, innate behaviors such as sucking, blinking, and crying become more complex behaviors. Behaviors are organized in the brain in mental patterns Piaget called "schema" (singular) or "schemata" (plural). Schemata in the brain can be likened to filing drawers or filing folders.

For example, when a person learns to ride a bicycle, it is possible that he is building upon prior knowledge ascertained when he learned to ride a tricycle, and riding a tricycle may have been based upon information obtained when he learned to ride a scooter. In Piaget's terminology, through the years, this person would have formed schema or schemata related to riding certain devices such as tricycles and scooters. As he built that schema and added behaviors to it, he was adapting to his environment through what the Piagetians called "assimilation" or activities that children participate in that help to bend and fit additional information into the knowledge and skills that they already have. When a completely new activity is encountered, such as changing batteries in a flashlight or using a rod and reel, children must "accommodate" new information and create a new schema or new file folder. Accommodation occurs when previously held notions are changed to fit new behaviors, thus creating a new schema or schemata.

Our youngest grandchild, Anne Marie, age 18 months, liked to put everything she encountered into her mouth. Piagetians would say she was assimilating—using tried and true behaviors for whatever she picked up. Food went into her mouth; blocks went to her lips; and she chewed the stuffed rabbit, sucked the pacifier, and tasted her dad's shoe. However, when she encountered an object that was unpleasant or that did not fit into her mouth, then she was forced to accommodate or to create a new pattern of behavior concerning the object she encountered. According to Piaget, if the only thing humans did was "assimilate," the brain would remain in a state of equilibrium, and little or no learning would take place. But when forced through encounters with the environment to accommodate, the brain enters a state of disequilibrium and accommodates the new information until equilibrium again is attained. Piaget said this process of equilibrium or disequilibrium occurs hundreds of times a day, which results in learning.

Piaget proposed that every person goes through 4 separate qualitatively different stages of cognitive development:

(1) The *sensorimotor* stage lasts from birth to 18 months or 2 years. During this time children use the senses and motoric activities to construct their own reality from the materials provided by the environment. The primary task accomplished is referred to as "object permanence" meaning that children are able to understand that an object they are familiar with exists, even though they do not actually see the object at the moment.

(2) The *preoperations* stage covers ages 2-7. During these years children learn to use symbols in their thought and communication. Their vocabularies expand tremendously, and they are able to continue the construction of their own reality through the materials they find in the environment. Children at this age experience the world especially through play, emphasizing what Piaget meant by preoperations.

(3) The *concrete operations* stage lasts from approximately 7-11 years. To Piagetians, operations are internalizing mental actions that allow children to work with more concrete problem solving rather than relating to the world primarily through physical actions. Children of this age are beginning to think logically, meaning they can classify objects and organize data into workable sets. They can learn rather complex material as long as the information is placed into the context of some experiences they have already had. For example, children of this age can understand certain concepts in history and social studies, such as wars, as long as teachers demonstrate what battles are, how they are fought, the strategies used, and the reasons for the conflicts. If these rather complex and abstract ideas are placed into the children's past experiences (using props, models, or other images), then learning can occur.

(4) When children reach the adolescent years, 12-15 years, they should be able to perform *formal operations*, meaning they should be able to think more abstractly and to solve problems in a highly systematic manner.

Perhaps Piaget's greatest contribution to the study of human development has to do with his insistence that children think qualitatively different from adults. This idea he dramatized through his 4 cognitive developmental stages.

In summary, infants and toddlers confront their environment through their senses and motoric operations. Preschoolers deal with environmental stimuli primarily by reacting to it physically (they run, jump, play, build, construct, and imagine). During later childhood and early adolescence children learn to reason logically about concrete events and to organize and classify information, although they are not yet able to deal with abstract information such as algebra, world history, theology, philosophy, and certain scientific studies. Formal operations occur when adolescents are able to reason in abstract and logical ways. Thought is idealistic and does not necessarily require prior experience in order to understand that a concept is possible. Thoughts "take wings," meaning there are no parameters on thinking.

Many developmentalists today point out that Piaget's thesis that children think qualitatively differently from adults is valid. Piaget did, however, tend to underestimate the cognitive ability of young children and to overestimate the cognitive ability of young adolescents.

Information Processing

Information processing scientists often use the computer as a metaphor to describe how human beings learn and perform. They say that humans are who they are and do what they do because of the way information is processed. They further postulate that the human brain is wired to gather and process information and that the older individuals become and the more experiences they record, the better processors of information they become. The information processing theory works like this:

• Information is taken into the brain from the physical world.
• The sensory register receives the information.
• Some information is retained, and a great deal of stimuli is permanently lost.

Piaget's Theory

The human organism is born with the tendency for:

ORGANIZATION (within the brain) AND ADAPTATION (to the environment)

ASSIMILATION
represents schemata present at any given time past or present

ACCOMMODATION
the process by which cognitive structures are modified

EQUILIBRIUM
a state of being in harmony with the environment

DISEQUILIBRIUM
a state of being out of harmony with the environment because current structures are inadequate for purposes. The trigger mechanism for intellectual development, occurring when existing cognitive structures do not work and accomodation is necessary, leads to new or augmented schemata.

REFLEXES
natural actions that form first, such as sucking, reaching, grasping, and blinking

SCHEMA
a cognitive structure that "holds" things associated

CONTENT
the behavior contained in a schema or schemata

COGNITIVE STRUCTURE
the number of schemata available to humans at any given time

ORGANIZATIONAL ABILITY
varies at different stages of cognitive development

* Piaget believed that all organisms had an innate tendency to maintain harmony with their environment. This concept accounts for motivation in intellectual development. Therefore, new cognitive schemata are generated through disequilibration, and disequilibration/equilibrium is a continuous growth process.

Piaget's Stages of Cognitive Development

Piaget's theory was expressed through four qualitative, universal, invariant stages

STAGE I	STAGE II
Sensorimotor birth-2 years Children construct their reality by engaging the environment with their senses and motoric actions.	**Preoperational** 2-7 years Children use one-way thinking, being fooled by form rather than substance, centering on only one aspect of a problem, and assuming everyone else experiences the world as they do. Operations are actions that can be reversed mentally and not just physically. The explosion of language and use of symbols is a first step toward operational thinking.
STAGE III	**STAGE IV**
Concrete Operations 7-11 years Children can analyze a problem from the end to the beginning and vice versa and can group objects into categories and sequences. Most thinking is bound to personal experiences.	**Formal Operations** 11-15 years Children can consider abstract possibilities, forming hypotheses and using deductive or inductive reasoning to solve problems. Thinking goes beyond personal experiences to using new information.

• Retained information is processed in the short-term or working memory.
• Retained information is rehearsed, elaborated on, organized, and used for decision making and other functions.
• Data stored in the long-term memory may be recalled or used later.

Executive control processes such as attention, strategy selection, monitoring, and expectations are directly involved in the entire information processing paradigm, from the sensory register to the long-term memory. Information processing scientists see the brain as active and constantly involved in transforming information, reducing information, elaborating on information, storing and recovering information, and, finally, and most importantly, using information to make decisions and to solve problems. Information processing theorists who use these concepts as a human development theory stress maturation and the accumulation of experiences. Theoretically, a 4-year-old will not be as adept at making decisions as an 8-year-old. Due to brain maturation and experiences, the more people age, the more expert they are in processing information. Maturation improves the speed at which information can be processed and the amount of space available for information.

Memory research stresses the importance of prior knowledge in presenting new or complex information. It appears that the brain's long-term memory stores related information into webs, networks, or schemata and, when new information can be connected to existing data in those sites, communication is enhanced.

Moral Development Theories

Jean Piaget spent the majority of his professional life studying the cognitive developmental aspects of children but did engage in some significant research in social processes, specifically moral development. He delighted in observing children at play. As he observed children on the playground shooting marbles and participating in other games, he concluded that children's interpretation of rules of the game changed as they grew older (in accordance with his cognitive developmental theory that older children become more sophisticated in their thinking). Children younger than 10 or so view rules as absolute and external; they are handed down by older children and/or adults.

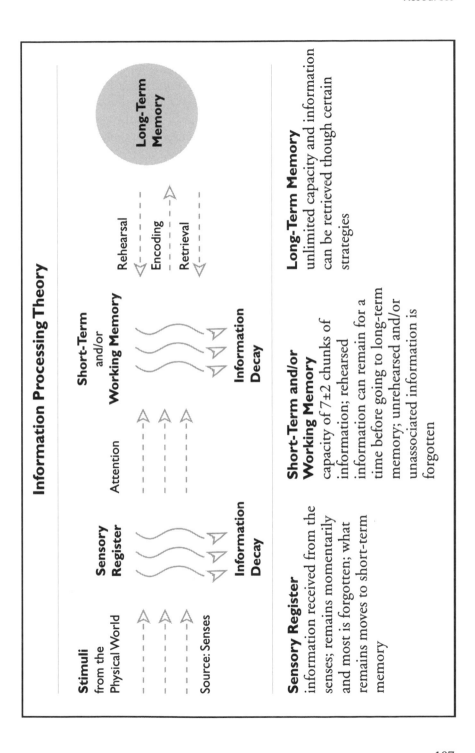

Information Processing Theory

Stimuli
from the
Physical World

Sensory Register

Attention

Short-Term
and/or
Working Memory

Rehearsal

Encoding

Retrieval

Long-Term Memory

Source: Senses

Information Decay

Information Decay

Sensory Register
information received from the senses; remains momentarily and most is forgotten; what remains moves to short-term memory

Short-Term and/or Working Memory
capacity of 7±2 chunks of information; rehearsed information can remain for a time before going to long-term memory; unrehearsed and/or unassociated information is forgotten

Long-Term Memory
unlimited capacity and information can be retrieved though certain strategies

Young children perceive rules as real and not to be changed. Piaget called their propensity for seeing rules as sacred the "morality of constraint" or "moral realism." Further, children in this age group have no sense of intent; the degree of guilt is related to the severity of the consequences. For example, if Brittany's brother spills a gallon of orange juice, it is more serious than spilling a cup of juice. Another example includes 5-year-old Justin whose mother has a rule that says "no eating 2 hours before dinner." But Justin's 12-year-old brother, Ben, has a snack an hour before dinner because he feels weak and is getting sick due to not eating since 10:00 AM Justin will not hear any of his brother's "excuses." The rule is the rule and the intent is not in Justin's perceptive ability—yet. On the other hand, Ben is at another cognitive stage and is able to see what rules are for and has little problem "stretching" rules and even making up new rules for old situations.

Piagetians call this ability to see rules as necessary but flexible the "morality of cooperation" or "autonomous morality." Piaget's explanation of the development of morality makes it easy to understand why young children and older children do not often play well together. Also, it increases awareness that young children sometimes break rules because they do not understand them.

Lawrence Kohlberg (1927–1987), a Harvard University professor of psychology and education, spent his relatively short professional life studying children's moral reasoning skills and became a leading authority in the field. His research subjects were primarily male, and his work centered on his subjects' ability to appraise certain posed "moral dilemmas" or moral issues on the basis of the justice perspective. By "justice," Kohlberg meant individual rights. This moral judgment theory proposes 3 levels and 6 stages.

Kohlberg contended that children's cognitive growth is qualitative in nature and that they progress in orderly fashion through Piaget's 4 cognitive developmental stages. A comparison of Piaget's stages of cognitive development with Kohlberg's paradigm reveals the importance of cognitive processes in Kohlberg's works.

Kolberg's thesis is that the more sophisticated a person's thinking is, the higher the level of moral reasoning. And the better individuals can reason morally, the more morally they will behave.

While Kohlberg's stages are sequential and invariant, there are, however, several factors that can influence the development of moral reasoning. Cognitive development is necessary, but alone, it is not sufficient for moral development to occur. Role-playing, life experiences, and hearing and seeing advanced moral reasoning practiced by others enhance the individual's own moral development. Age, as related to stage, is not a critical factor to Kohlberg or to many stage theorists. Periods of human development and age levels are included in the interpretive charts as guidelines for the reader.

Kohlberg's Theory of Moral Development

Level	Stage	Moral Perspective
Preconventional Morality	1. egocentric view	emphasis upon punishment and obedience.
	2. compliance view	emphasis upon gaining rewards by complying with rules—concrete
Childhood		thinking
Conventional Morality	3. approval of others	being seen by others as a "good boy" or a "good girl"
	4. maintaining social order	follows rules and respects authority—believes in the
Adolescence		system
Postconventional Morality	5. social contract	believes in the will of the majority and the rights of others
	6. universal moral principles	a strong internalized personal code of ethics based on universal moral
Adulthood		principles

Carol Gilligan (b. 1936), professor of human development and psychology at Harvard University, was a student of Kohlberg's and says that Kohlberg's research was flawed due to his use of primarily male research subjects. She projects a moral developmental model based on the "care perspective," which stresses interpersonal relationships and connectedness as opposed to Kohlberg's emphasis upon individual rights (justice perspective).

Gilligan's claim that males are socialized to become more concerned about individual rights and that females are more centered on feelings for others (care perspective) has some research support, but there is also evidence that both genders can process moral feelings for others and strive for positive interpersonal relationships.

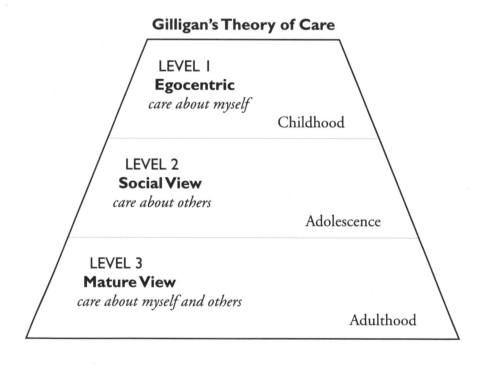

Gilligan's Theory of Care

LEVEL 1
Egocentric
care about myself
Childhood

LEVEL 2
Social View
care about others
Adolescence

LEVEL 3
Mature View
care about myself and others
Adulthood

Sociocultural Theories

Uri Bronfenbrenner

Uri Bronfenbrenner's (b. 1917) theory of human development stresses a strong ecological view. Bronfenbrenner's theory consists of 5 environmental systems ranging from the microsystem—the family, the school, peers, neighborhood, health, and church groups—to the macrosystem—the attitudes and ideologies of the culture. In the microsystem developing children have some direct input into their reality and environment, but in the macrosystem they have little or no input. Bronfenbrenner's point is that society helps to shape the development of children and to some degree children help to shape the environment in which they live. Bronfenbrenner's research has brought to center stage in developmental psychology the bidirectional effects of children and their environment.

Lev Vygotsky

Lev Vygotsky was born in 1896 (the same year as Piaget) into an intellectual Russian Jewish family. He died in 1934 of tuberculosis. During his short lifetime he received an extraordinary education and made a profound impact on the field of developmental psychology. Vygotsky was schooled in literature, linguistics, social science, philosophy, medicine, law, and psychology.

Although Vygotsky's view of cognitive development is similar to Piaget's, he emphasized the social construction of knowledge, whereas Piaget emphasized the individual acquisition of knowledge by each child. Vygotsky's theory is a contextualist theory, meaning that humans can be understood only in their social context. Children, then, are inherently active social beings who live and exist in a system of interacting forces from the past, present, and future. Therefore, they know what is imparted to them from those with whom they are in contact. Vygotsky's view of human development follows a dialectical process of thesis, antithesis, and synthesis.

One of Vygotsky's most utilitarian ideas is what he called the "zone of proximal (nearby) development." The zone of proximal development describes what children can do by themselves (baseline) and what they can do with assistance from someone who is older and more knowledgeable. According to Vygotsky, the zone refers to any situation in which an activity is leading children beyond their current level of thinking. Some refer to this idea as scaffolding. Vygotskians would say that effective teachers are those

Bronfenbrenner's Ecological Theory

Microsystem
the relationship between the child and her immediate environment

Mesosystem
the relationships between and among the institutions and services in the child's immediate environment

Exosystem
the accumulation of the culture's institutions and services that affect the child indirectly

Macrosystem
the attitude, beliefs, and ideologies of the culture

who present material to children that is just slightly ahead of children's baseline information. In this context, intelligence would mean that it is not what is known now but rather what can be known with help. Vygotsky would say that the cognitive activities of thinking, remembering, and attending occurred first between individuals and later within the individual's mind. To this school of thought intellectual function must first appear between two minds before it becomes internalized into one's mind.

This notion that social activity shapes the mind of children is a uniquely different view from Western cognitive psychology, which stresses individual cognition. Although Vygotsky's theory is aimed primarily at a collectivistic society and is primarily based upon the economic and philosophical views of Marx and Engles, it is a useful theory because it stresses the sociocultural context of human development and integrates everyday learning and development.

Humanistic Theories

Carl Rogers

Carl Rogers (1902–1987) was known for his theory of client-centered or person-centered therapy. In terms of the human developmental paradigm, Rogers believed that if children are reared with "unconditional" love, they will grow to be competent, productive, and secure individuals. If, on the other hand, children are reared in situations where caregivers place conditions on love, they will grow up to be anxious, insecure, and perhaps even neurotic and psychotic. In other words, "unconditional" love produces positive mental health, and "conditional love" produces individuals who are mentally unhealthy. Unconditional love insists that "I will love you no matter what"; conditional love offers, "I will love you if . . ." Persons reared in conditional love environments grow up with unhealthy concepts of themselves and others. Rogers said that children must hold themselves in esteem before they can adequately cope with the changes of life. His ideas about self-concept and self-esteem have had extraordinary influence in schools, churches, government, and indeed all aspects of the culture.

Abraham Maslow

Abraham Maslow (1908–1970) was perhaps best known for his hierarchy of needs model that explains a hierarchical range of needs from lowest to highest. The lowest level of needs, such as safety and security, are necessary in order for higher needs, such as enrichment and eventually self-actualization, to be realized. This model is extraordinarily useful in explaining some of the behaviors of children. For example, it is unreasonable to think that children will learn such concepts as sharing, thoughtfulness, kindness, and helpfulness if they are in home situations in which they are threatened, abused, starved, and neglected. Parenthetically, it is also foolish to believe that most children will be in a mood to learn reading, writing, math, and spirituality if their basic needs such as food, shelter, and safety are not met. (Perhaps that is why schools have food programs and enrichment programs for their students, and why churches have feeding, clothing, and housing programs.)

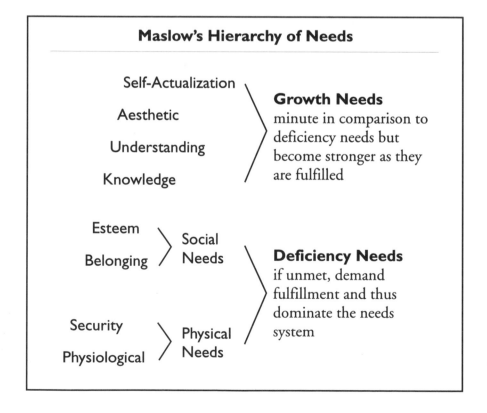

Maslow's Hierarchy of Needs

Self-Actualization

Aesthetic

Understanding

Knowledge

Growth Needs
minute in comparison to deficiency needs but become stronger as they are fulfilled

Esteem

Belonging

Social Needs

Security

Physiological

Physical Needs

Deficiency Needs
if unmet, demand fulfillment and thus dominate the needs system

Faith Development Theories

James Fowler

James Fowler (b. 1940) has expanded the thinking of Piaget, Erikson, and Kohlberg into the spiritual domain. Through formal studies and informal observation Fowler pondered the meaning and impact of faith in the lives of individuals. Beginning in 1972, while on staff at Harvard University, he conducted empirical research on his theory that faith develops in stages. From this longitudinal study came Fowler's theory of faith development, which has become the recognized paradigm in this area of study.

In order to understand Fowler's theory of faith development, one must first understand Fowler's definition of "faith." In both his writings and in interviews Fowler is explicit in his clarification of how he interprets faith. In the introduction to his book, *Stages of Faith,* Fowler wrote:

> I believe that faith is a human universal. We are endowed at birth with nascent capacities for faith. How these capacities are activated and grow depends to a large extent on how we are welcomed into the world and what kind of environments we grow in. Faith is interactive and social; it requires community, language, ritual, and nurture. Faith is also shaped by initiatives from beyond us and other people, initiatives of spirit or grace. How these latter initiatives are recognized and imaged, or unperceived and ignored, powerfully affects the shape of faith in our lives.

Faith, says Fowler, is a way of knowing, construing, or interpreting one's experience. This concept implies that faith is dynamic, active, changing, and growing. There is an unbreakable weaving of cognition and effectivity in faith. In fact, Fowler states he consciously tried to avoid the separation of cognition and emotions.

Perhaps most important in Fowler's definition of faith is the understanding that faith is a dynamic way of giving meaning to life. Faith is the way humans find and make significance in their lives. Therefore, it incorporates the processes of knowing, feeling, valuing, understanding, experiencing, and interpreting. Because everyone searches for meaning or significance, Fowler also contends that faith is universal. This quest for meaning misses no one; without some sense that life is meaningful, individuals live neither long nor well. Faith, then, is not necessarily religious; it can just as easily be centered on a career, family, success, or even oneself.

Religion, with its accumulation of past traditions, provides patterns for present and future generations. Religion, however, is not synonymous with faith. Nor is the understanding of the word "belief" synonymous with faith. Belief can be a way of communicating faith, but faith is deeper than belief. Fowler itemizes each of these ideas to stress his major point: faith is dynamic, interactive, and social. It is not a passive word, but active, a word that connotes engagement and fluidity. At the same time it is universal. Every human being has faith, and Fowler theorizes that faith develops in certain sequential stages that, while not necessarily age-related, do occur in the same order for all individuals.

Following Piagetian structuralism, faith development theory emphasizes that the whole is greater than the sum of its parts. In other words, faith is much more than the information gathered from empirical interviews and scientific analysis. Structuralism also maintains that the parts of the whole are integrated, that a structure is an organized system of meaning within an individual's thought processes. These structures are dynamic, but the dynamic process is developmentally ordered.

Through this structuralist approach Fowler attempts to describe the predictable patterns of how faith matures. While this approach to faith development recognizes the interrelationship among structural, genetic, and functional aspects of development, it is most concerned with the individual's construction of meaning; the structure allows the prediction of the emergence of patterns even in the midst of change. Fowler's faith development theory depicts an order in development of a number of dimensions in which an individual's framework of understanding and valuing change through various stages.

In his study of the development of faith Fowler identified 7 stages that appear in a sequential, hierarchical order, regardless of the object of faith. These stages are not meant to be age-related, although there are some general age ranges given in which stages typically appear. The purpose of defining these stages, however, is not to judge where a person is or should be on any scale but to help identify what stage an individual may be in and what can generally be expected in that stage and the next to come. Piaget, Erikson, Kohlberg, and Fowler found that there are enduring ways of constructing thoughts and beliefs that remain constant for varying periods or stages in life. The transition to the next stage begins when maturation and experiences cause discord in existing systems and when new structures are needed to deal with reality. Speaking of these stable periods and transitions in terms of stages best describes the picture Fowler is trying to portray.

Fowler's stages of faith development begin while the child is still in utero. The first stage of *primal faith*, which Fowler calls a pre-stage because it is inaccessible to empirical research and is influenced by the psychological health of the mother during pregnancy. After the birth of the infant, this stage continues approximately through the first year of life as the child experiences his environment, and specifically as a bond is established with his parents or caregivers. Obviously, the family is instrumental in the nurturing that takes place in the primal faith stage. The way that parents or their substitutes communicate assurance of life's meaning and purpose, both verbally and non-verbally, establishes the foundation for the development of a more formal faith in succeeding years. A mutuality occurs between parent and child, even while the child is in this pre-language stage; the child forms a predisposition to trust based on the rituals of care offered by his parents. The child's development of early trust and faith enables him to endure later separations from his parents without undue anxiety.

The influence of both Piaget and Erikson can readily be seen in the emphasis on the development of trust and in Piaget's definition of infant development as a sequence of cognitive and emotional stages. Even though Fowler considers this period as undifferentiated, or pre-stage, its importance to faith development cannot be overemphasized. What happens to the child at this stage sets the tone for all the experiences that will occur as life progresses.

Next in Fowler's faith development theory is the *intuitive/projective* faith stage that spans the early childhood years. It begins as the child learns to speak and use language. The thought processes at this stage are fluid and largely self-centered. Because this is a highly imaginative stage, the child is particularly influenced by stories, symbols, and gestures that combine with perception and feeling to create lasting faith images. These images represent both the protective and threatening powers surrounding the child and are shaped by the prominent adults in her life. Childhood images or representations of God take form during this stage, and the child is highly influenced by experiences with her parents and other significant adults with whom she has had an emotional attachment.

The stage of intuitive/projective faith also corresponds to the awareness in the child of good and evil as his moral standards and emotions develop. The connection with Lawrence Kohlberg's conventional level of moral reasoning is obvious. As the conscience develops, the child struggles to maintain a balance of autonomy with shame, much as Erikson outlined in his second crisis. Unable to think logically at this stage, the child's imagination and feelings govern the way he sees the world. There is little distinction between fact and fiction; the affective domain is in control. Thus, knowing and feeling tend to be intermingled. Fowler points out that parents and other sources of authority should be especially careful not to present excessive moralizing, as stories of this nature can terrorize the child and have lasting detrimental effects.

The last stage of childhood proper is called the *mythic/literal* stage. The emergence of concrete operations in thinking as outlined by Piaget permits the child to think logically and to arrange her world in some kind of order. Faith is mythic at this stage because the child can now grasp life-meaning in stories, but most understanding is limited to concrete thinking. Therefore, the stage is also a literal period. Literal thinking may limit the way the child can contemplate and respond to biblical truths, but the important understanding for this stage is for the child to be able to separate fantasy from reality. The use of narrative through stories, drama, or other methods can help her sort the real from pretend and bring coherence to her experiences.

A child in the mythic/literal stage is beginning to develop the ability to see things from the perspective of others and can make his own meaning from the biblical stories he hears. Because the child is typically concerned about the groups to which he belongs (family, church, school), he is also interested in the lore of these groups. It is, therefore, an important time to share biblical stories and stories of family and religious traditions. A child's concept of God may be that of a stern but loving supernatural being who keeps a scorecard of who is to be forgiven and rewarded and who is to be punished. When a child realizes God does not work this way, s/he may undergo what Fowler terms "11-year- old atheism."

Fowler's term actually denotes a crisis of faith within the child who cannot yet think in the abstract and understand the concept of an invisible yet sovereign God. As the child tries to reconcile her thoughts and experiences relating to God, a temporary turning away from childhood faith may occur. This implicit clash in understandings will lead her to a reflection on meanings. By early adolescence, as the transition to Piaget's formal operational thought begins, the child will regard God once again as a loving being who is interested in overcoming pain in the world. This transitory time prepares the child for the next phase of faith development.

The remaining stages of Fowler's faith development deal with individuals in adolescence and adulthood. The *synthetic/conventional* faith stage witnesses the emergence of a strong relational component as a youth sees himself in relationship with others. Because of this relational ingredient, a sense of belonging to a community is important. Values and beliefs from earlier stages are synthesized into a coherent whole, but the resulting perspective is typically representative of the larger community to which the individual belongs. In other words, the individual in the synthetic/conventional faith stage tends to adopt the values of his particular community, often due to an underdeveloped awareness of the faith of any group except his own.

The *individuative/reflective* faith stage is typically experienced during young adulthood. There is critical reflection upon one's own values and beliefs with an understanding of the self as part of a larger social system, while also assuming the responsibility for making ideological choices. This stage is individuative in the sense that a person now establishes her own identity after critical reflection, and the stage is reflective in that there is a conscious thinking about the values and practices of the group.

The *conjunctive* faith stage deals with the many polarities of life and strives to maintain a sense of balance and coherence while wrestling with the tensions that arise. There is an awareness and questioning of self and judgments made in the individuative/reflective stage, while recognizing that others may have different insights. This may lead to a search for new understandings through interactions with a variety of faith groups.

Universalizing faith occurs only after the individual has experienced a radical submission of self into oneness with God. The person who is in the universalizing stage of faith cares little for the things of this life, and yet cares much for the people he meets in life. His focus is on love and justice, with no room for oppression or divisions. It is the rare individual who attains this stage. Placed in the paradigm of Fowler's benefactors, Piaget would say this stage represents formal operation thinking; Erikson would call this universalizing faith integrity; and Kohlberg would point to his postconventional level, stage 6 universal ethical principle orientation. In addition, Fowler's universalizing faith is akin to Maslow's self-actualization.

Fowler's Stages of Faith Development

STAGE	AGE	ACTIVITIES/OUTCOME
Undifferentiated or Primal Faith	conception-2 years	• bonding with caregivers • mutuality between child and caregiver • predisposition to trust established
Intuitive/ Projective Faith	2-7 years	• illogical thinking • knowing and feeling intermingled • imagination and feeling govern
Mythic/Literal Faith	7 years-adolescence	• symbols, attitudes, and rules perceived literally • God is seen as concrete • believe in "an eye for an eye"
Synthetic/ Conventional Faith	adolescence-young adulthood	• adopt values and beliefs of groups to which they belong • accept authority of trusted leaders without analysis • interpersonal relationship with God
Individual/ Reflective Faith	young adulthood	• critical analysis of personal belief system • religious symbols examined • understanding and acceptance of others' beliefs
Conjunctive Faith	adulthood	• intellectual restlessness • questioning of self and judgments made in past • organization of personal truth into new configurations
Universalizing Faith	adulthood	• possess feeling of oneness with humankind and deep love of God • care little for "things of this life" • focus is upon love and justice

John H. Westerhoff, III

John H. Westerhoff, III (b. 1933), a noted author on faith development, echoes Fowler's reasoning in the definition of the word faith. Faith is of necessity active, according to Westerhoff. It is a deeply personal matter, but it is also evidenced in behavior. Faith is expressed daily in interactions with other people.

Therefore, faith cannot be taught through the usual methods of instruction; it must be experienced. This area is where faith differs from religion, and where, in Westerhoff's assessment, the church has fallen far short of its duty to nurture faith in the next generation. Because religion can be taught, the ideas and models of schooling and formal instruction have been emphasized to teach religion in Christian education. The passing of faith to children, however, must involve more than classroom instruction in Bible content, church history, or beliefs. The transfer must include a process, a way of experiencing how a person of faith thinks and acts. Involvement and participation in the process are essential, even for children. The "teaching" of faith is better done, therefore, through persons within the community of faith modeling and sharing their faith.

By Westerhoff's definition, characteristics of a community of faith are simple and succinct. They include:

- a clear identity and agreement of what is believed
- a suitable size to maintain meaningful, purposeful interactions among members
- the presence and interaction of three generations
- unity of all roles among diversely gifted persons

It is the third of these components that makes Westerhoff's key point. If faith is to be taught in the community of faith, that community must contain an intergenerational presence. There must be interaction among and between the three generations, each of whom represents an era of time. The older generation represents memory, without which it is impossible to pass on faith. The middle generation symbolizes the present, whose responsibility it is to keep reality before the community. The younger generation is emblematic of the future, and thus, the vision for the community of faith. Only when all generations are participants in the traditions and rituals of the community, including worship, can faith be transmitted. This important piece of Westerhoff's paradigm is highly reminiscent of aspects of the extended family of primitive cultures in which the older generation preserves and passes on memory, the middle generation provides the essentials of life, and the younger generation provides hope for the future.

Participation in these rituals requires some preparation. Faith education can be enhanced if the lessons to be proclaimed during the formal worship hour are linked to age-appropriate experiences and discussions beforehand. Individuals learn best by first learning through experience, then through stories that magnify those experiences, and finally through language that explains the stories and the experiences and links them all together conceptually.

Westerhoff diverges from Fowler's stages of faith as he develops a series of *styles* through which faith can expand. These 4 styles are generally found at the ages Westerhoff notes, but not everyone reaches all these styles. It is not uncommon for persons to attain the characteristics of one style and never move to the next. However, the 4 possible styles, as described by Westerhoff, are:

• *Experienced faith*—This is the foundation of faith and is generally experienced in the preschool and early childhood years. The interrelationship between language and experience is emphasized, as faith is expressed through interactions with others. The experiences children have in connection with words of faith lead to an experienced faith as they share with and are influenced by others in the faith community.

• *Affiliative faith*—The need to identify with and participate in a community of faith characterizes the late childhood and early adolescent years. Nurture in and a sense of belonging to a community of faith leads to the internalization of the community's values.

• *Searching faith*—The ability to grow in faith typically occurs during the years of adolescence. Reminiscent of Fowler's "11-year-old atheism," the person who is in the style of searching faith questions and typically discovers for himself the truth of the faith once taken for granted. When this period of questioning is resolved, the individual is ready to move to the last of Westerhoff's 4 styles.

- *Owning faith*—Occurring at the end of the adolescent years or at the beginning of early adulthood, owning faith is a defining moment. Likened by Westerhoff to conversion, owning faith constitutes a major change in a person's thinking, feeling, and willing. Faith has been explored personally and embraced individually. The person who is in the style of owning faith can now commit herself to the lives of other people or to worthy causes.

As children and adults in all of these styles share stories, experiences, and worship, faith is nurtured and passed on to the next generation. The language used, the stories shared, and the presence of a mixture of generations work together to make it possible for children to have faith.

David Elkind

David Elkind (b. 1931) is another child developmentalist who focuses on issues directly related to religion and faith of children. He conducted a study with 300 Protestant children between the ages of 6 and 14 years in which subjects were asked questions regarding their religious denomination. These questions attempted to ascertain when children are able to conceptualize the characteristics common to all Protestants and when they realize that persons may belong to more than one group at the same time. The results of this study indicate that these understandings develop in 3 age-related stages. A brief overview of the stages described in Elkind's book, *The Child's Reality* follows.

- *Stage 1*—Children have a basic conception of meaning. They have a vague, confused conception of class-membership compatibility. At this stage they only know that denominational terms refer to persons.

- *Stage 2*—From the ages of 7-9, the prayer concept emerges for the first time. At this stage children rise above the actual behaviors associated with prayer and begin to understand its mental and affective aspects. The most important characteristic of this stage is the abstraction of concrete referent properties of denominational terms.

- *Stage 3*—Children between the ages of 10 and 12 show a new level of thinking. At this stage they no longer look for evidence of religious identity in the person's outward behavior but instead look for it in a person's innermost beliefs and convictions.

It is of utmost importance, according to Elkind, for adults to be inclusive and considerate of a child's reality. He says that children are most like adults in their feelings and least like adults in their thoughts. Elkind refers to this focus on adult needs as *adult egocentrism*. It is only when children are treated like adults in their feelings but different in their conception of reality that the chains of misunderstanding between children and adults begin to be broken.

Effective communication is essential for breaking the chains of misunderstanding. Communication between adults and children necessarily requires adults to understand how children think and speak. Children up to the adolescent years think in literal, concrete terms. When this understanding is applied to the spiritual development of children, one must make a conscious effort to speak in the language of children. Adults responsible for the spiritual training of children within the church setting must be familiar with the stages of childhood physical, cognitive, socioemotional, moral, and faith development in order to understand how to relate religious terms to the realties of the children's lives.

Children in the early childhood years think very literally. This holds true in their spiritual development and in other dimensions of growth. In discussing how children build their faith, for example, K. Kantzer describes a 5-year-old boy who suddenly began misbehaving for no apparent reason. When the mother talked with her son about his behavior, the boy told her he had heard that if you are good, then when you die you will go to be with Jesus in heaven. What he understood, however, was if you are good you will *die*—and go to be with Jesus in heaven. He definitely was not ready to die, so he determined to be as bad as possible! The symbols and rituals used in church can easily confuse children who interpret things so literally. Therefore, the words and deeds used to explain faith must be chosen carefully. Adhering to Piaget's stages of cognitive development, most children are not able to understand intangible or abstract matters, including God, until they reach the age of early adolescence.

Personal Theories

Most people have fashioned their personal theory of human development out of their own experiences. That theory may not have academic labels attached, but it is a theory of how people grow and develop nevertheless. For example, some people subscribe to the term "bad seed," meaning that a person is born bad due to genetics (mom or dad was bad), and they will always be bad. This theory would be referred to academically as an extreme genetic or biological view. The theory that "this child is not ready" is also a biological or maturational posture, as is "the acorn does not fall far from the tree."

Then there are those with the human development view that is best expressed as "you are who you associate with." These folk would be in the extreme learning theory group. They believe that you are whatever your environment teaches you. The theorists who subscribe to the belief that "you are the master of your destiny" would be more accepting of the cognitive developmental theories of Piaget and information processing. Those who accept the idea that "she was reared in a horrible home situation and never had a chance" would be more akin to the psychoanalytic theories of Freud and followers. Likewise, persons who theorize that "children shape their environment and the environment shapes them" are more attuned to ecological and/or sociocultural theories. Finally, there is this viewpoint from the humanistic canon: "All that really matters is what you think of yourself."

Most individuals have formulated their personal theories of how people got to be the way they are through experience. But even small children will amaze adults with their insights about why someone is doing what they're doing or why somebody will succeed or not. Consider the 8-year-old who said of his friend, "Boy, Tom is a worker; he is going to be great!"

There are several basic philosophical questions encountered and eventually answered on the way to formulating personal theories of human development. Those questions have to do with freedom, the nature/nurture debate, individuality and personality, independent actions, and view toward life.

- Are people basically free to control their own behavior, or is behavior predetermined?
- Are individuals a collection of genes, or does environment play the major role?
- Are individuals totally unique, or do they possess similar characteristics that are somewhat universal in nature?
- Do individuals primarily act on their own initiative, or do they just react to stimuli from the environment?
- Are human beings basically optimistic or pessimistic?

The answers to these philosophical questions and others like them basically help form personal and rather eclectic theories of human development. A study of the formal academic theories assists in augmenting and evaluating every individual's own personal theory.

Current Children's Sermon Research

Although most of the research relating to children's sermons has been conducted in connection with graduate school dissertations, there is much yet to know about the appropriate use of this teaching method within the worship experience of children. In an effort to know more about the use in mainline Protestant churches, a study was conducted during the 1997–1998 academic year.

The primary purpose of this study was to investigate, by use of a survey, the extent to which the Episcopal, Presbyterian USA, Southern Baptist (SBC), and United Methodist (UMC) denominations in Florida, Georgia, Texas, and Virginia use children's sermons in the Sunday morning worship service. The purposes of children's sermons in these denominations and the materials and methodologies used in the delivery of them were also studied.

The 12-item questionnaire (see p. 128) was designed so that respondents were forced to choose one answer for each question. There was no allowance for multiple primary purposes, methodologies, and sources of information for children's sermons.

In surveying the literature, little research was available on the subject of children's sermons. Most of the research focusing on the advantages of including a children's sermon in the corporate worship service has been conducted by candidates for the Doctor of Ministry degree within their own church congregations, thus limiting the scope of the study and application of the results. My survey was broader based, including 21,867 churches.

Hypotheses/Assumptions

In keeping with the research method, some necessary hypotheses and assumptions were made, namely:

Hypotheses

• Children's sermons will be used in the morning worship services of mainline Protestant denominations in the southern United States. The children who participate will be 4-9 years of age.

Children's Sermon Survey February 9, 1998

I am conducting research on the children's sermon. The children's sermon is defined for this survey as an established time during the Sunday A.M. worship service devoted exclusively to children. The children do not leave the sanctuary for this sermon. This questionnaire will take approximately 3 minutes to complete. If you are not the person directly responsible for the children's sermon, please refer this survey to the appropriate person with a request that they complete the questionnaire and return it to me in the enclosed self-addressed, stamped envelope by February 23, 1998.

Please check the appropriate box for each question (1 answer per question). Your answers are confidential.

1. **Denomination:** ❑ Baptist (SBC) ❑ The Episcopal Church ❑ Presbyterian (USA) ❑ United Methodist

2. **Person completing survey:** ❑ Senior Minister/Associate Minister ❑ Education Minister
   ❑ Children/Youth Minister ❑ Music Minister ❑ Other (please specify)

3. **Current church membership size:** ❑ less than 100 ❑ 100-500 ❑ 501-1000 ❑ 1001+

4. **Location of church:** ❑ rural ❑ village or small town ❑ medium size town/small city ❑ metropolitan area

5. **How long has your church had a children's sermon in the Sunday A.M. worship service?**
   ❑ 5 or more years ❑ 2-4 years ❑ 1-2 years ❑ less than 1 year ❑ 0 years (no children's sermon)

If you selected 0 years for question 5, stop here and return the survey. If you selected any other answer, please complete questions 6-13.

6. What is the *primary* **purpose of the children's sermon in your church? Please check only one answer.**
   ❑ help children become acclimated to the routine of the worship hour
   ❑ help children understand that the worship hour includes them along with the "big people"
   ❑ introduce children to the symbols, language, structure, and meaning of the church
   ❑ teach the fundamental principles of theology
   ❑ witness to children for the purposes of salvation and church membership

7. **Where did you learn your information about children's mental, physical, and social development? Please check only one answer.** ❑ college, seminary, graduate study ❑ personal experience (reading, conferences)
   ❑ other (please specify)_____

8. **How many credit courses in child development or related subjects (such as Educational Psychology, Theology for Children, Child and Family Development) have you completed in college, seminary, or graduate school?** ❑ 0 ❑ 1-2 ❑ 3-5 ❑ 6 or more

9. **At what age do children typically begin participating in the children's sermon?**
   ❑ 2 ❑ 3 ❑ 4 ❑ 5 ❑ 6 or above

10. **At what age do children typically** *stop* **participating in the children's sermon?**
    ❑ 5 ❑ 6 ❑ 7 ❑ 8 ❑ 9 ❑ 10 or above

11. **Where do you obtain** *most* **of your material for the children's sermon? Please check only one answer.**
    ❑ actual stories from the Bible ❑ books or magazines that illustrate biblical teachings
    ❑ personal experiences that show biblical truths

12. **What primary presentation methodology do you use in the delivery of the children's sermon? Please check only one answer.** ❑ demonstration using visual aids, manipulatives, or gifts to children
    ❑ storytelling ❑ question and answer

Comments:

- There will be no differences in the purposes, methodologies used, or sources of information for children's sermons within mainline Protestant denominations in the southern United States.

Assumptions

- No significant differences occur between the sample selected and the overall population.

- The sample included a slightly larger percentage of Episcopal and Presbyterian churches than was actually represented in the population due to the requirement of at least 30 churches in each denomination responding to the survey.

- Respondents answered questions on the survey objectively.

- There are no differences in how respondents understood and responded to survey questions.

- Respondents are in a similar type of church structure with similar background and training.

- Those completing the survey have a similar context in which to interpret the survey's questions.

Random Sample

The sample selected consisted of a stratified random sampling of the population and included 49 Episcopal, 65 Presbyterian, 288 Southern Baptist, and 142 United Methodist churches for a total sample of 544. Within each denomination the number of churches selected by state was based upon that state's percentage of the total population. Concern over the size of the Episcopal and Presbyterian populations when compared with the overall population led me to select a higher percentage of churches within these denominations to participate in this study. The increase in the Episcopal and Presbyterian churches selected resulted in a slight overrepresentation of these two denominations (3.66% versus 2.29% of the Southern Baptist and

United Methodist denominations) when compared to their percentage of the total population. This decision was made with the assumption that this difference in representation would not significantly change the sample, and that it would ensure, with a 70% return ratio, a satisfactory number of questionnaires for data analysis.

Population by Denomination and State

Denomination	State			
	Florida	Georgia	Texas	Virginia
Episcopal Church	342	161	441	370
Presbyterian Church USA	376	305	566	524
Southern Baptist Convention	2368	3238	5446	1537
United Methodist Church	838	1623	2130	1602

Survey Questionnaires

Prior to the distribution of the final questionnaire, a pilot study was conducted involving 57 churches in the selected denominations within the central Georgia area in order to eliminate any confusing items and provide a formative evaluation of the questionnaire. Necessary corrections and refinements were then made, and the revised questionnaire was mailed to the sample of 544 churches along with a self-addressed, stamped envelope.

After the requested return data had passed, letters and self-addressed, stamped envelopes were mailed to nonresponding churches in the sample. Because less than 70% of the surveys were returned after the second notice, phone follow-up became necessary. Phone interviews were conducted with 16 of the nonresponding churches and added the information gleaned from them to the data received from responding churches, and then compiled into a database to allow for efficient data analysis.

A total of 262 surveys were returned. Of these surveys, 153 indicated an established time in the Sunday morning worship service devoted exclusively to children. While all demographic information was considered for statistical analysis, only those conducting children's sermons were required to complete the remainder of the questionnaire. In the statistical analysis, questions were eliminated that contained multiple or no responses.

Because less than 70% of the surveys were returned, care must be taken in interpreting the results. The number of surveys returned (262), however, was adequate for making inferences and drawing reasonable conclusions despite the lower than desired percentage of returns.

One-dimensional chi-square analyses were performed to determine levels of significance of each question. These analyses also provided descriptive information about the churches that responded to the survey. A stratified random sample was drawn to maintain the proportions of the subgroups within the population. The patterns of survey return for all denominations closely represented the proportions identified in the sample.

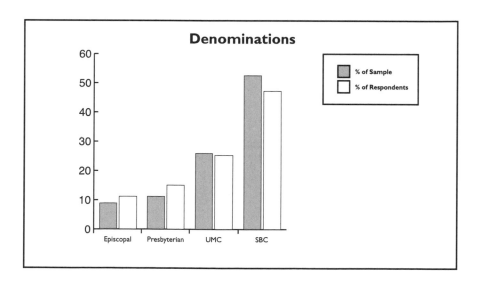

Several questions on the survey were designed to elicit demographic information about the churches.

Question 3 asked for the size of the current church membership. Of the respondents, a significant number of churches reported a membership of less than 500.

- 30.9% indicated a membership less than 100.
- 46.2% reported a membership of 100-500.
- 14.5% reported having 501-1000 members.
- 7.6% indicated memberships of more than 1000.

Question 4 concerned the location of the churches. There was an even distribution of respondents among all geographic locations.

- 26% were located in rural areas.
- 24% were located in villages or small towns.
- 25.6% were located in medium size towns or small cities.
- 22.5% were located in metropolitan areas.

Three survey questions requested information about the person who conducts the children's sermons. Only those churches that indicated they include a children's sermon in the morning worship service were examined in the statistical analysis. They report the following information concerning the presenter:

- 57%-the minister or associate minister
- 13%-the children's or youth minister
- 7%-education
- .01%-music minister
- 18%-"other" (volunteers, Sunday school directors/teachers, coordinators and directors of Christian education)

Two questions asked specifically about the background and training of the person responsible for presenting children's sermons. Respondents report they received their information from the following sources:

- 56.2%-child development courses at college, seminary, or graduate school
- 32.7%-personal experience
- 4.6%-other

132

Respondents were also asked to identify the number of credit courses in child development or related subjects they had completed in college, seminary, or graduate school. The majority of the respondents reported having 1 or more such courses.

- 25.5% reported 1-2 courses.
- 26.8% reported 3-5 courses.
- 22.9% reported 6 or more courses.
- 21.6% reported no courses.

The remainder of the questions on the survey were directly related to the children's sermon. Significant levels of difference (p.<.05) were calculated for 5 of these 6 questions. Chi-square values and levels of significance for each of these questions are summarized in the following chart.

Children's Sermon Survey Results			
Survey Item	Chi-Square Analysis	df	p level
Part of Worship Service			
Overall	7.389	1	p<.01*
Denominations	21.973	3	p<.001*
Primary Purpose	64.489	4	p<.001*
Beginning Age	45.457	4	p<.001*
Ending Age	262.237	5	p<.001*
Information Sources	.097	2	p<.10
Primary Presentation Method	39.362	2	p<.001*
*Significant findings			

Research Results

The results show that children's sermons are a part of the Sunday morning worship service; these results are significant at the $p < .01$ level. The results were further analyzed with a two-dimensional chi-square analysis across denominations and found to be significant at the $p < .001$ level. Greater numbers of United Methodist churches reported having children's sermons than those that reported not having children's sermons; this was the primary contributing factor to the significance level reached for this question. The following graph shows the percentage analysis across denominations of whether the children's sermon is a part of the Sunday morning worship service. It is important to note that, although the Presbyterian percentages resemble those of the United Methodists, the United Methodists returned a larger number of surveys, thereby having a greater impact on the results.

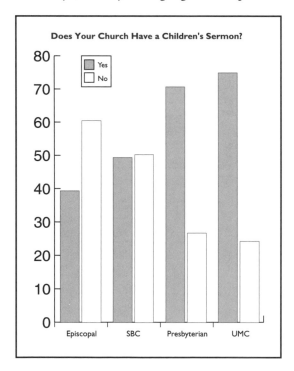

Of the 153 churches using children's sermons, 139 (90.8%) identified a single primary purpose as directed on the survey. The following graph reflects a percentage analysis of only these responses.

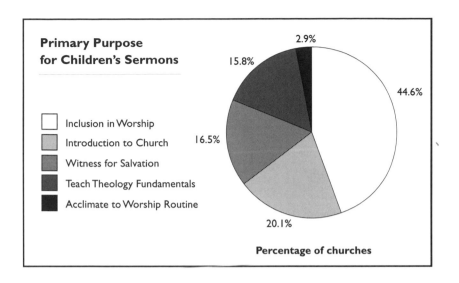

Primary Purpose for Children's Sermons

- Inclusion in Worship
- Introduction to Church
- Witness for Salvation
- Teach Theology Fundamentals
- Acclimate to Worship Routine

2.9%
15.8%
44.6%
16.5%
20.1%

Percentage of churches

Analysis

The chi-square analysis of these figures reveals significant differences in the primary purpose of children's sermons in church; the results are significant at the level of p<.001. Fewer churches than expected indicated their primary purpose for children's sermons was to help children become acclimated to the routine of the worship hour. A greater number than expected indicated their primary purpose was to help children understand that the worship hour includes them along with the "big people." These results had the greatest impact on the level of significance found for this question.

Also significant at the p<.001 level are beginning and ending ages of those attending children's sermons. Significantly more churches than were expected reported that children begin attending the children's sermon at the age of 3 years. A significant number of churches also reported that children typically stop attending at 10 years or above. These two responses had the greatest impact on the significance levels reached for these questions. As seen in the following graph, approximately 1/3 of churches reported that children begin attending the children's sermon at age 3, while almost 2/3 reported that 10 years or above is typically the age when children stop attending

Results were also significant at the p<.001 level for the primary method of presentation used in the delivery of children's sermons. The primary contributors to this level of significance were those respondents who indicated

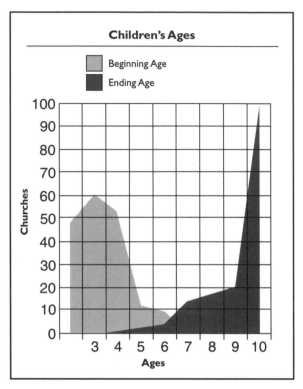

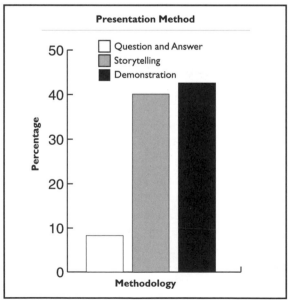

they use demonstrations with visual aids, manipulatives, or gifts to children, along with those who reported the use of storytelling as their primary method of presentation.

Discussion and Summary

Respondents were asked to complete a structured questionnaire in order to ascertain the prevalence and design of children's sermons in mainline Protestant denominations in the southern United States. Of the 6 questions that pertained directly to children's sermons, 5 revealed significant results. The results support the hypothesis that children's sermons are included as part of morning worship services. While the results also support the hypothesis that children from the ages of 4-9 years attend children's sermons, they also suggest that children begin to participate at a younger age (2) and continue to attend past the age of 9 (10 or above).

The results of the survey indicate there are significant differences in the purposes and methodologies used in the delivery of children's sermons. Thus, these tenants of the hypothesis are contradicted. Findings reveal, however, there are no significant differences in the sources of information presenters choose in preparation for children's sermons, with results evenly spread among the choices of actual Bible stories, literature that illustrates biblical teachings, or personal experiences that show biblical truths. While purposes and methodologies vary, the findings of this study show that the children's sermon is a method for including children in the corporate worship service in mainline Protestant denominations in the general geographical area known as the Bible Belt.

This wide range of ages of participants in children's sermons necessitates detailed preparation for this worship experience. Knowledge of child developmental theories should govern the planning and delivery of children's sermons. According to the results of this study, 78% of respondents indicated they have completed at least one course in child development theory. Thus, presenters report having some exposure to the knowledge base needed to successfully conduct children's sermons. The extent to which this knowledge is used in preparation for children's sermons is beyond the boundaries of this study.

The results of this research suggest presenters may encounter a group of children ranging in age from 2-10 or older. Present within this group are children who have just begun to speak and use language and who are egocentric and highly imaginative. At the opposite end of the spectrum are children who are beginning to understand the perspectives of others but are still limited to concrete thought processes.

As a part of planning for children's sermons, one must consider the primary purpose for conducting them. Results of this study indicate a significant number of churches view children's sermons as a means to help children understand that the worship hour includes both themselves and the "big people." This finding is consistent with C. R. Case and others whose prior research concluded that children's sermons can make children feel important to and included in the faith community. With many churches reporting a wide range of ages who attend children's sermons, it would seem this primary purpose serves all children who desire to participate.

Prior research also shows that children's sermons can teach fundamental principles of theology. However, only 14.4% of respondents to the current study chose this as their primary purpose for children's sermons. In previous research W. T. Medlin, III, studied children ages 6-10, and C. R. Case studied children ages 4-9. These investigations did not encompass the wide range of ages found in the current study to participate in children's sermons. Therefore, whether children's sermons can successfully teach children from 2-10 years of age the fundamental principles of theology is unproved and should be considered in future research. Due to the abstractness of theological concepts, however, developmental theory would cast doubts on the positive outcome of such a study.

Approximately 1/3 of respondents to this study indicated other primary purposes for which no research base exists. These purposes include helping children become acclimated to the routine of the worship hour; introducing children to the symbols, language, structure, and meaning of the church; and witnessing to children for the purposes of salvation and church membership. Because of the absence of previous research, it is unknown whether these purposes can be accomplished through children's sermons. These are questions to which future research should also be directed.

In addition to the primary purpose, presenters should also consider the presentation method that will be used for children's sermons. The results of this study indicate that presenters prefer storytelling or demonstrations using visual aids, manipulatives, or gifts to children as their primary method of presentation. Significantly fewer respondents chose the question-and-answer model. This is not surprising since the literature reveals that discussion type sermons are particularly challenging due to the unpredictable nature of children.

As stated earlier, there has been little research to date relating to children's sermons. Studies that have been completed have been narrow in focus, primarily concentrating on one church or denomination. In such an atmosphere, generalizations cannot be made to larger populations. The current study contributes broad-based research across denominations with valuable insight into what children's sermons encompass and how they are incorporated into worship services.

This research provides a strong foundation for both future investigation and this book. The survey design limited respondents to one selection per question. This single response does not account for the possibility of multiple purposes, methods, and sources of information and does not provide an overall picture of the multifaceted worship experience for children. Future research should allow respondents to identify or rank all elements involved in planning and delivering children's sermons. Observational research can also expand the current study to provide a more complete picture of the design and structure of children's sermons.

Further study is also needed to solidify the ages of the children participating in children's sermons. The current study found a wide range of ages, thus contradicting the current literature, and gives rise to the question of the ability of presenters to adequately deliver a message with meaning for all children. In addition, several questions must be asked:

- Do presenters plan for the developmental levels of the children?
- Do presenters have different purposes within the same sermon to benefit all of the children who participate?
- Do presenters communicate in a way that all children understand?

Other research should also address the issue of methods of presentation of children's sermons. Empirical research is needed to establish the best method or methods of presentation. Questions to be considered include:

- Do children benefit from sermons that employ the storytelling method?
- Do children benefit from an object lesson even when they are unable to transfer their knowledge of concrete objects to abstract moral lessons?

The theories of child development have been broadly applied to the development of faith in children. In order for churches to adequately serve the children in their congregations, they must craft methods of presenting the essential elements of faith to them.

References and Suggested Readings

Books

Astley, J. "Faith Development: An Overview." In *Christian Perspectives on Faith Development: A Reader*, edited by J. Astley and L. J. Francis, xvii-xxiv. Grand Rapids: Wm. B. Eerdmans, 1992.

Bandura, A. *Social Learning Theory*. Englewood Cliffs NJ: Prentice Hall, 1977.

_____. *Social Foundations of Thought and Action: A Social Cognitive Theory*. Englewood Cliffs NJ: Prentice Hall, 1986.

Chamberlain, G. L. *Fostering Faith: A Minister's Guide to Faith Development*. Mahwah NJ: Paulist Press, 1988.

Coleman, R. J. *Gospel-Telling: The Art and Theology of Children's Sermons*. Grand Rapids: Wm. B. Eerdmans, 1982.

Cully, I. V. *Christian Child Development*. San Francisco: Harper & Row, 1979.

Downs, P. G. "The Power of Fowler." In *Nurture That Is Christian*, edited by J. C. Wilhoit and J. M. Dettoni, 75-90. Wheaton IL: Victor Books, 1995.

Elkind, D. *Child Development and Education: A Piagetian Perspective*. New York: Oxford University Press, 1976.

_____. *The Child's Reality*. Hillsdale NJ: Lawrence Erlbaum Associates, Inc., 1978.

_____. *The Hurried Child*. Rev. ed. Reading MA: Addison-Wesley, 1988.

Erikson, E. H. *Childhood and Society*. 2d ed. New York: W. W. Norton & Co., 1950.

_____. *Identity: Youth and Crisis*. New York: W. W. Norton & Co., 1968.

_____. *Toys and Reasons: Stages in the Ritualization of Experience*. New York: W. W. Norton & Co., 1977

Fowler, J. W. "Life/Faith Patterns: Structures of Trust and Loyalty." In *Life Maps: Conversations on the Journey of Faith*, edited by J. Berryman, 14-101. Waco TX: Word Books, 1978.

_____. *Stages of Faith: The Psychology of Human Development and the Quest for Meaning*. San Francisco: Harper & Row, 1981.

_____. *Becoming Adult, Becoming Christian: Adult Development and Christian Faith*. New York: Harper & Row, 1984.

_____. "Strength for the Journey: Early Childhood Development in Selfhood and Faith." In *Faith Development in Early Childhood*, edited by D. A. Blazer, 1-36. Kansas City MO: Sheed and Ward, 1989.

_____. "The Vocation of Faith Development Theory." In *Stages of Faith and Religious Development: Implications for Church, Education, and Society*, edited by J. W. Fowler, K. E. Nipkow, and F. Schweitzer, 19-36. New York: Crossroad Publishing Co., 1991.

_____. *Weaving the New Creation: Stages of Faith and the Public Church.* NY: HarperCollins, 1991.

_____. "Faith, Liberation, and Human Development." In *Christian Perspectives on Faith Development: A Reader,* edited by J. Astley and L. J. Francis, 3-14. Grand Rapids: Wm. B. Eerdmans, 1992.

_____. "Perspectives on the Family from the Standpoint of Faith Development Theory." In *Christian Perspectives on Faith Development: A Reader,* edited by J. Astley and L. J. Francis, 320-44. Grand Rapids: Wm. B. Eerdmans, 1992.

Freud, S. *A General Introduction to Psychoanalysis.* New York: Washington Square Press, 1917.

_____. *The Complete Psychological Works..* Edited by J. Strachey. London: Hogarth Press, 1953.

Gallagher, J. M., and D. K. Reid. *The Learning Theory of Piaget and Inhelder.* Monterey CA: Brooks/Cole Publishing Co., 1981.

Gay, L. R. *Educational Research: Competencies for Analysis and Application.* 5th ed. Upper Saddle River NJ: Prentice-Hall, 1996.

Gesell, A. *An Atlas of Infant Behavior.* New Haven CT: Yale University Press, 1934.

Gilligan, C. *In a Different Voice.* Cambridge MA: Harvard University Press, 1982.

Gilligan, C., J. V. Ward, J. M. Taylor, and B. Bardige, eds. *Mapping the Moral Domain.* Cambridge MA: Harvard Univeristy Press, 1988.

Gorman, J. A. "Children and Developmentalism. In *Nurture That Is Christian: Developmental Perspectives on Christian Education,* edited by J. C. Wilhoit and J. M. Dettoni, 141-58. Wheaton IL: Victor Books, 1995.

Hanson, R. S. *Worshiping with the Child.* Nashville: Abingdon Press, 1988.

Heller, D. *The Children's God.* Chicago: Univeristy of Chicago Press, 1986.

Hendricks, W. L. *A Theology for Children.* Nashville: Broadman Press, 1980.

Juengst, S. C. *Sharing Faith with Children: Rethinking the Children's Sermon.* Louisville KY: Westminster/John Knox Press, 1994.

Kohlberg, L. *Essays on Moral Development: Vol. I. The Philosophy of Moral Development: Moral Stages and the Idea of Justice.* San Francisco: Harper and Row, 1981.

Lee, J. M. "Christian Religious Education and Moral Development." In *Moral Development, Moral Education, and Kohlberg,* edited by B. Munsey, 326-59. Birmingham AL: Religious Education Press, 1980.

Lester, A. D. *Pastoral Care with Children in Crisis.* Philadelphia: Westminster Press, 1985.

Lorenz, K. Z. *Evolution and the Modification of Behavior.* Chicago: University of Chicago Press, 1965.

Maslow, A. *Motivation and Personality.* 2d ed. New York: Harper and Row, 1970.

Moseley, R. M., D. Jarvis, and J. W. Fowler. "Stages of Faith." In *Christian Perspectives on Faith Development: A Reader,* edited by J. Astley and L. J. Francis, 29-57. Grand Rapids: Wm. B. Eerdmans, 1992.

Neal, C. J. "The Power of Vygotsky." In *Nurture That Is Christian*, edited by J. C. Wilhoit and J. M. Dettoni, 141-58. Wheaton IL: Victor Books, 1995.

Nelson, C. E. "Does Faith Develop? An Evaluation of Fowler's Position." In *Christian Perspectives on Faith Development: A Reader*, edited by J. Astley and L. J. Francis, 62-76. Grand Rapids: Wm. B. Eerdmans, 1992.

Osmer, R. R. *A Teachable Spirit: Recovering the Teaching Office in the Church*. Louisville KY: Westminster/John Knox Press, 1990.

Parks, S. D. "The North American Critique of James Fowler's Theory of Faith Development." In *Stages of Faith and Religious Development: Implications for Church, Education, and Society*, edited by J. W. Fowler, K. E. Nipkow, and F. Schweitzer, 101-15. New York: Crossroad Publishing Co, 1991.

_____. "Faith Development in a Changing World." In *Christian Perspectives on Faith Development: A Reader*, edited by J. Astley and L. J. Francis, 92-106. Grand Rapids: Wm. B. Eerdmans, 1992.

Piaget, J. *Reasoning and Judgment in the Child*, translated by Warden. Totow NJ: Littlefield, Adams, & Co., 1976.

_____. "The Theory of Stages in Cognitive Development." In *The Learning Theory of Piaget and Inhelder*, edited by J. M. Gallagher and D. K. Reid, 199-209, translated by S. Opper. Monterey CA: Brooks/Cole Publishing Co., 1981. Reprinted from *Measurement and Piaget*, edited by D. R. Green, M. P. Ford, and G. B. Flamer. New York: McGraw-Hill, 1971.

Rest, J. "Developmental Psychology and Value Education." In *Moral Development, Moral Education, and Kohlberg*, edited by B. Munsey, 101-30. Birmingham AL: Religious Education Press, 1980.

Rogers, C. R. *Client-Centered Therapy: Its Current Practice, Implications, and Theory*. Boston: Houghton Mifflin, 1951.

_____. *On Becoming a Person*. Boston: Houghton Miffin, 1961.

Rupp, A. N. *Growing Together: Understanding and Nurturing Your Child's Faith Journey*. Newton KS: Faith & Life Press, 1996.

Santrock, J. W. *Children*. 5th ed. Dubuque IA: Brown & Benchmark Publishers, 1997.

Skinner, B. F. *The Behavior of Organisms: An Experimental Analysis*. Englewood Cliffs NJ: Prentice Hall, 1938.

_____. *Science and Human Behavior*. Englewood Cliffs NJ: Prentice Hall, 1953.

_____. *Verbal Behavior*. Englewood Cliffs NJ: Prentice Hall, 1957.

Smith, W. A. *Children Belong in Worship: A Guide to the Children's Sermon*. St. Louis: CBP Press, 1984.

Steele, L. L. "The Power of Erikson." In *Nurture That Is Christian: Developmental Perspectives on Christian Education*, edited by J. C. Wilhoit and J. M. Dettoni, 91-103. Wheaton IL: Victor Books, 1995.

Stonehouse, C. "The Power of Kohlberg." In *Nurture That Is Christian: Developmental Perspectives on Christian Education*, edited by J. C. Wilhoit and J. M. Dettoni, 61-74. Wheaton IL: Victor Books, 1995.

_____. *Joining Children on the Spiritual Journey: Nurturing a Life of Faith*. Grand Rapids: Baker Books, 1998.

Westerhoff, J. H., III. *Values for Tomorrow's Children: An Alternative Future for Education in the Church*. Philadelphia: Pilgrim Press, 1970.

_____. *Will Our Children Have Faith?* New York: Seabury Press, 1976.

Wright, J. E., Jr. *Erikson: Identity and Religion*. New York: Seabury Press, 1982.

Journals

Butcher, C. J. "Symposium: Children's Sermons." *The Christian Ministry* (January 1982): 13, 18.

Carr, J. A. "The Children's Sermon: An Act of Worship for the Community of Faith." *Perkins Journal* 36, no. 3 (1983): 1-57.

Coleman, R. J. "Beyond Moralism: Children's Sermons Should Bring Good News Rather Than Grand Expectations." *Reformed Worship* 12 (1989): 10-13.

Dillard, P. "Children and Worship." *Review and Expositor* 80 (1983): 261-70.

Fowler, J. W. "Fowler on Faith." *Christianity Today* 30 (13 June 1986): 71-81.

_____. "Toward a Developmental Perspective on Faith. *Religious Education* 69 (1974): 207-19.

_____. "Gifting the Imagination: Awakening and Informing Children's Faith." *Review and Expositor* 80 (1983): 189-200.

Grimes, G. "Teaching the Bible to Children." *Review and Expositor* 80 (1983): 221-30.

Kantzer, K. "Building Faith: How a Child Learns To Love God." *Christianity Today* 30 (13 June 1986): 41-151.

Smith, M. U., and O. S. Sims, Jr. "Cognitive Development, Genetics Problem Solving, and Genetics Instruction: A Critical Review." *Journal of Research in Science Teaching* 29 (1992): 701-13.

Thurston, N. S. "Shame and Guilt in Christian Children: Interventions with Projective Techniques and Play Therapy." *Journal of Psychology and Theology* 22 (1994): 377-82.

Microfilm

Case, C. R. "An Investigation into the Functional Value of the Children's Sermon within the Framework of the Morning Worship Service." Ph.D. diss., Eastern Baptist Theological Seminary, 1982. *Dissertation Abstracts International* 43, no. 03, 0829B. University Microfilms No. AAI8219449.

Dunbar, T. A. "The Children's Sermon: Can the Minister's Awareness of Child Development Principles Strengthen This Experience?" Ph.D. diss., Drew University, 1982. *Dissertation Abstracts International* 43, no. 09, 3025A. University Microfilms No. AAI8302394.

Medlin, W. T., III. "Exploring How Children and Their Parents Respond to Various Means of Children's Participation in Worship." Ph.D. diss., Drew University, 1986. *Dissertation Abstracts International* 47, no. 06, 2192A. University Microfilms No. AAI8616760.

Stillings, G. D. "Children's Sermons: Communicating with the Congregation." Ph.D. diss., Boston University, 1985.

Youngblood, S. D. "Inclusiveness: The Incorporation of Elementary-Age Children in the Total Morning Worship Experience: Development, Implementation, and Evaluation of an Educational Model for St. John's United Methodist Church, Georgetown, Texas." Ph.D. diss., Perkins School of Theology, 1992.

Other

Lawrence, L. "Stages of Faith." *Psychology Today* 17 (November 1983): 56-62.

Lewis, J. L., C. J. Maholski, and A. L. Moliere. "Inclusion of Children's Sermons in the Worship Services of Mainline Protestant Demoninations." Master's project, Mercer University, 1998.